# LEE MARTIN

**BOOKCRAFT**
SALT LAKE CITY, UTAH

All characters in this book are fictitious,
and any resemblance to actual persons,
living or dead, is purely coincidental.

Library of Congress Catalog Card Number: 97–72090

ISBN 1–57008–315–0

First Printing, 1997

Printed in the United States of America

*This one is especially for Lorraine Szczesny, who goes after diagnoses the way Deb goes after murderers; and for her nurse, Richelle Fletcher, who can always make me laugh. There is much to be said—all favorable—about a physician and medical team who actually listen to their patients.*

# To My Readers

Several years ago I began to feel that St. Martin's was no longer the best house for my Deb Ralston series. Recent developments have enabled me to move this latest installment to Bookcraft, as I had hoped to do. The change has given me the liberty to work with much more of what I want to develop in Deb Ralston's life. I hope that you will like the results.

Anne Wingate
writing as
Lee Martin

# MID-OCTOBER TO
# FRIDAY, NOVEMBER 12

# 1

CURTIS MINOT HAD LITTLE ENOUGH to smile about. His retirement plans, which had included fishing, hunting, sailing, and other active sports, had been raggedly shredded when the boom on his sailboat struck him—hard—in a sudden squall on Lake Texoma. As he contemplated a life of no movement and no feeling below the waist, he still wasn't sure whether he was really grateful to the stranger who had dived in to save him.

But all the same he was alive, and once he had passed the near-madness that had darkened the first year, he realized that he would protect even this half-life with all the strength he had in him. *I'm a survivor,* he told himself fiercely, over and over. *I land on my feet.*

But he wasn't on his feet now, or even in the detested wheelchair that was presently shoved into a corner. This was the manual one, with the wheels he turned with his hands; the motorized one was kept downstairs. He wouldn't—couldn't— get up until Jeanne came to help him, not unless he wanted to slide out of bed and then slither on his stomach, pulling himself with his arms—not that he wouldn't do that, not that he hadn't done that a few times already. His arms were stronger than ever, to make up a little bit for the uselessness of his legs.

Usually if she went out before he was up she remembered to put the wheelchair beside his bed, so that, using those strong arms, he could swing himself into it and do the few things he could do for himself. But this time she'd forgotten.

He'd called her a couple of times but she hadn't answered.

She must have left early, to go with that gaggle of women she jogged with every Thursday. She'd said she would, he remembered—something about one of the women having to go to work early. "The Thursday Club," they called themselves, with much laughter that sometimes included him only because a woman he scarcely even knew, a woman named Deb, spoke to him as casually, as naturally as she did to anyone else, if he happened to be downstairs when the women entered together.

Sue would include him if she knew how, but she didn't: since his injury, it was as if his twin sister had become a stranger. And that was odd, considering how close they'd always been. They even looked alike in some ways. He was big, six feet three inches tall, broad-shouldered, and heavy-built, though he'd never been fat before his life reduced itself to sleeping, sitting, and eating; and she was much smaller, a full head shorter than he, and slender. Always had been slender and still was. But their coloring was the same, hair that sandy red-blond the English call ginger, green eyes, freckles. Sue's face was oval and his was square, but their noses were just alike, and their eyes were so alike that some people, ignorant of the fact that only same-sex twins can be identical twins, had thought when they were children that they were identical.

Of course they weren't alike; they didn't think at all alike, and Sue would be horrified if she knew the source of the money that had paid for his house, his luxuries, and hers as well, because her husband, Ken, for whom he had named his own son, had worked with him for years before getting scared and changing his line of work.

He chuckled grimly, and then coughed. He'd been coughing a lot lately; Jeanne wanted to take him to the doctor, but he didn't want to go. He'd had enough of doctors.

His mind wandered back to Sue and her probable reaction to the way he made his money. Let her be horrified. It was no skin off his nose. And at least she still *tried* to include him as a person.

Jeanne wouldn't include him.

Not by her own choice.

Not his beautiful, petite, slender Jeanne, with the laughing brown eyes and the short black curly hair, the body like a pocket Venus and the perfectly oval, clear olive face like a Renaissance princess.

Not anymore, though before the accident she had constantly sought his presence. Not anymore, though when they were both awake and alone she dutifully attended to the personal matters he was constantly humiliated by his inability to attend to himself; at their meals together—and she continued to insist that they eat together, as if to maintain the fiction that life was normal—she dutifully chatted mindlessly. She tried to tell him she still loved him; she tried to tell him it was just his morbid imagination convincing him otherwise; but he knew what he knew.

Jeanne had what she wanted, all she wanted from him now: his money, his nominal presence, and minimal demands from him. One nurse arrived at ten A.M. and the second relieved that one at six P.M. Only from two A.M. till ten A.M. did Jeanne have the responsibility of his care, and presumably he spent that time sleeping, just as she did.

He didn't, not much. Sleep was increasingly elusive. And no wonder; what did he do to tire himself? What *could* he do? Swim a little, using his arms, hardly more than a dead man's float? Clean the guns he could no longer take hunting, tie flies for the fishing trips he could no longer take? What was he supposed to do?

Read? Watch television?

Learn to play wheelchair basketball?

Not much for a man who had been in the prime of his life.

Even pain could have reminded him he was alive. But even that negative sensation was denied him.

He had little enough to smile about.

But he smiled now.

The jangle of Polka's rabies, registration, and identification tags against the metal buckle of his collar was ascending the stairs. He and Jeanne had laughed about that when they first got Polka. "We'll never have to wonder where he is," Jeanne had said.

The Dalmatian, then two years old, had done about as much to save his life as had the stranger who had dived from a nearby boat into Lake Texoma's chilly waters to drag him out. Polka's presence had mattered especially in those early days, when Curtis was still trying to come to grips with the catastrophe and still thinking, a little more every day, about suicide. He could have left everything else. But somehow he couldn't quite leave Polka.

Now Polka was four years old, and Curtis didn't think often about suicide.

That was just as well, because he had to have his handgun close enough he could reach it, even now, even retired and paraplegic, even in his own bedroom. There were too many people who wanted to kill him. That wasn't paranoia; that was fact.

The jangling continued along the hall, coming toward his room. But something was odd, Curtis thought, using his arms to push himself a little higher up in the bed. He could hear the tags, but he couldn't hear the clicking of Polka's toenails on the hardwood floor.

He was still wondering why that was, when the door was nudged open.

He expected to see Polka's black nose pushing around the door.

But that wasn't what he saw. "What the— Dog collar in your hand— Are you out of your mind— *What are you doing?*"

He didn't wait for the obvious answer; he just lunged for the semiautomatic pistol in the bedside table.

And didn't have time to reach it.

The last cough wasn't very loud.

# 2

---

October 11

TO:       Roberta Harris, M.D.
          <u>VIA FAX</u>
FROM:     Deb Ralston
RE:       Medical Advice, Following of

(1)  Broiled  fish  is  all  right  without  tartar
sauce.
(2)  One  cup  of  boiled  eggplant  is  definitely
enough,  even  with  onions  and  lemon  juice.  But  it
takes two cups of squash to be enough.
(3)  Fat-free  salad  dressing  is  not  all  right,  but
low-fat  is.  But  fat-free  mayonnaise  works  just  fine
for binding tuna salad together.
(4)  Butter Buds on corn on the cob work very well.
Yogurt and Butter Buds work okay on baked potatoes.
(5)  I'm jogging again. Okay? Can we not talk about
my  weight  anymore  till  next  year?  After  all,  it's
not  but  twenty  pounds.  All  right,  thirty.  But  it's
not  two  hundred  or  anything  like  that.  It's  just
that  I  never  started  jogging  again  after  Cameron
was born, and that was five years ago and that just
adds up to six pounds per year and anyway, I'll lose
it. I promise.

# 3

---

Friday November 12 1800 hrs.

TO:      Chief of Police
VIA:     Captain Millner
FROM:    Deb Ralston
RE:      Why I needed a veterinarian at a homicide

(Captain—I'll make a formal report later. This is just an explanation for the chief. Millie, give the captain this copy so he'll know what was going on. Just type the part outside parentheses for the chief. I'll go back and insert parentheses here and there so you'll know what not to type for the chief.)

(My doctor was having forty fits about the weight I had gained.) [Millie, are you supposed to close parentheses at the end of every paragraph? Well, just do it however it's supposed to be done.]

(Anyway, so was Captain Millner. Unhappy about my weight, that is. So was Harry, for that matter. And I wasn't real pleased myself. ~~That's the problem with having a full-length mirror in the Never mind.~~ [Millie, maybe you'd better retype the part for the captain as well as the part for the chief. I'll put in brackets too, for notes to you. This would be easier to write if I had had more than three hours of sleep in the last thirty-six hours; I think my brain is in neutral.] Or else maybe it's flooded.)

(So anyway I was out jogging this one morning, okay, it was a Thursday morning, but it's been a couple of months ago now, because the captain *finally* let me take some of that comp time that keeps piling up, and I ~~ran into no, he'd take that literally, and I didn't literally.~~ ) ~~While reporting officer was out on a morning jog, I encountered~~ (Millie, figure out a way to say this for it to make sense to the chief. For the captain, just say I was out jogging one morning a couple of months ago and I remet Sue Rimer and met Jeanne Minot. I'd known Sue for a couple or three years—she and her husband bought the Masseys' house when the Masseys moved to Boston—and she told me Jeanne was her sister-in-law. What kind of sister-in-law . . . I know, he'll ask that. Okay, Sue is Jeanne's husband's sister, and Jeanne's husband, of course, is Curtis, Curtis being the victim. Jeanne and her husband Curtis bought a house about a block away from Sue and Ken after Curtis retired.)

(Okay, here's how we'll put it for the chief:)

Thursday morning at 0630 reporting officer went jogging with Sue Rimer, whom I'd known for several years, and her sister-in-law Jeanne Minot, whom I'd just met in September. We have been jogging together on Thursday morning for two months.

By appointment, we convened on a corner about two blocks from my house, and then we jogged a couple of miles out and a couple of miles back, keeping to back roads. (Millie—It was really good jogging weather, cool without being really cold, well, at least not cold after we'd been running a mile or so, and after we'd jogged the four—well, come to think of it, it must have been about five—miles we walked around the block a couple of times to cool off before we went in.) [Okay, more for the chief:]

By agreement, we'd take turns winding up at each other's houses for hot chocolate. (Actually, when it's at Sue's or Jeanne's house it's coffee but they always make me hot chocolate, and I just make hot chocolate for all of us when it's my turn.)

(And this morning we went jogging just as usual. I was supposed to be at work before ten because I might need to be in court, so we started out early, so Jeanne didn't bring Curtis downstairs before she left like she usually does because he was still asleep. We met at the corner about six-thirty, and jogged till about seven-thirty and then we went over to Jeanne's house because it was her turn for the chocolate and so forth.)

(Let's put it this way for the chief:)

Reporting officer had arranged with Captain Millner to take comp time every Thursday morning for jogging, but this week I had to be at the office by about nine-thirty because I have a case in court this week. So I talked with Sue and Jeanne on Wednesday night and we agreed to go early so that I would have time to eat and shower before going to court. This week we had agreed to go to Jeanne's house for chocolate and then Sue would drop me by my house.

When we arrived at the Minot house, Jeanne went upstairs to hang up her jacket and to ~~bring Curtis downstairs—they've got an elevator, she certainly couldn't push his wheelchair down the stairs, but he needs needed help getting into the wheelchair.~~ attend to her husband Curtis Minot, the victim. She normally helped him into his wheelchair and brought him down on his elevator before we went jogging, but this morning she left before he would have gotten up, so she went to attend to him immediately on our ~~ret~~arrival. When she went into the bedroom she ~~found him shot to death~~ discovered the body. ~~So of course she screamed and I went tearing up the stairs with Sue right behind me, and she—Jeanne, not Sue—was flipping out, and I got her into her bedroom—no, from what she says, she's a restless sleeper and was keeping him awake, and so they hadn't slept together since his accident.~~ She notified me of the situation and I immediately went to check on it.

Victim was lying on his back in bed, the top of his head pointed toward the west, with his upper torso and head propped up on a stack of pillows, dressed in ~~skivvies~~ underwear. He had what appeared to be a bullet entry wound in his left forehead. His right arm was hanging off the right side of the bed. A drawer adjacent to his right hand was partially open and contained an empty holster and a box of ammunition. On the floor below his right hand was a 9 mm Glock semiautomatic pistol. (Millie, get the SN from records. It's in my notebook but I left my notebook in the car.)

Victim's wife was totally hysterical and I first dealt with her, trying to get her into her own bedroom—victim and wife had not shared a bedroom since the accident—and securing the scene as best I could. ~~Then Jeanne bolted into the upstairs bathroom and started throwing up, not that she had much to throw up,~~ Victim's wife went to bathroom and began to ~~wretch~~ retch and she was screaming that he'd promised he wouldn't kill himself, she wouldn't have let him have the pistol if he hadn't promised ~~but it wasn't suicide. I can tell you that for sure.~~ not to kill himself. It appeared that some effort had been made to make the death appear to be a suicide, but ~~it definitely wasn't~~ such did not appear to me to be the case.

(Millie—Put the rest of this into officialese. I don't have the energy to think about it. Anyhow, Sue went and looked before I had time to stop her and then *she* wanted to throw up and she went tearing to a downstairs bathroom because Jeanne was still occupying the main upstairs one, and the next thing I knew *Sue* was screaming.)

(That was when I went charging back *down* the stairs, and there was that Dalmatian lying on the bathroom floor limp as a rug, but he was breathing. I went to try to pick him up to see why he was unconscious, in case that was relevant to the crime, and that was when I noticed his collar was twisted. [~~+~~Millie—It had been buckled like, you know, when you're making a Möbius strip and you take a long piece of paper and twist it once and then you can prove by making a continuous line that the paper now has only one side instead of two. Hal [you remember Hal, don't you? My son that's on his mission right now?] drove me crazy showing me that over and over when he first found out about it.)

This situation seemed so odd that reporting officer had reason to believe that the collar, and the dog's unconsciousness, were in some way related to the case.

So I picked the dog up, not touching the collar, and put him in the living room ~~before Sue had a chance to barf on him, except that by that time she had changed her mind and didn't need to barf anymore anyway.~~ where he was protected from bathroom traffic.

At that point reporting officer called headquarters to report the crime and told the dispatcher to ~~get me~~ summon necessary personnel including a medical examiner's team, a detective team, and also a veterinarian, who~~m~~ [Millie, is that *who* or *whom*?] I needed in order to determine what had caused the dog's unconsciousness and possibly determine the relationship between this and the homicide.

(Captain—I hope the chief is through being mad. He should have realized I wouldn't call a veterinarian if I didn't really need one.)

(Thanks, Millie.)

# II

## THURSDAY, NOVEMBER 11

# 1

WE WERE ALL LAUGHING WHEN WE went into the house. That's one part of it that I can't get out of my mind—we were laughing, but of course we knew no reason, then, why we shouldn't be laughing. We'd run our five miles and then walked a couple of blocks to cool down, but then, and I don't remember who suggested it, we'd decided to race from the corner to Jeanne's house. We all got there about the same time, slamming shoulders and hips against the elegant double front door with its shining brass on varnished and waxed natural wood. We continued laughing, and then Jeanne pulled her key ring out of her pocket and unlocked the front door—and yes, I heard the click as she turned the key, so I know it really was locked—and we piled into the living room, still laughing, and Jeanne turned and, as usual, punched in four numbers on a keypad by the door and we all saw the little light by the keypad turn from yellow to green. Taking her cap off and running her fingers through her hair, she said, "Good grief, it's cold in here!"

It felt warm to me, after all that running, but after I took off my jacket while Jeanne rushed to slam a kitchen window, I too could tell that it was cool and would certainly feel chilly to Curtis. "Can't imagine how I managed to leave it that way," Jeanne said. "I opened it this morning after I burned some toast, but I could have sworn I closed it." She paused, her elegant dark face looking puzzled. "Come to think of it, I thought it was a different window I opened. My brain must have been on strike—no wonder, considering I set off the intruder alarm when I opened the window, and scared myself out of ten years' growth!—and right now I better go up and check on Curtis." Another irresistible giggle bubbled out. "He'll want to know what all that noise was!"

That started us laughing again—though Curtis was not much older than my fifty-one years, he sometimes gave the impression of being a wise old dog watching us playful puppies—and Jeanne bounded up the stairs two at a time, tossed her jacket from the stair landing into her room, where it landed on her bed (I found out later), and then pushed open the door to Curtis's room. She called his name, still with laughter in her voice, and then she screamed.

The sound of that scream gave me a pretty good idea of what she was seeing, and I also went up the stairs two at a time, except that I wasn't laughing. I remember glancing down as I reached the landing to see Sue standing with her hand over her mouth, her face chalky, her head lifted up as if she could find a way to see into Curtis's room from downstairs. She was Curtis's sister. And she too must have guessed from the sound of Jeanne's scream, because she had headed for the stairs but I had reached them first, stumbling slightly at the landing and then running toward Jeanne, who was sprawled on her left knee, with her right leg stretched behind her, across Curtis's bed, shaking him with both arms, screaming, "Wake up, Curtis, please wake up, please, Curtis—"

I called her name and she looked frantically back at me, tears rolling unheeded down her face still rosy from jogging, and cried, "Deb, I can't wake him up! I can't make Curtis wake up!"

No. She couldn't. Nobody would ever wake him, not in this world. I approached the bed where she was still shaking him, took her by the shoulders, and pulled her toward me, saying, "Jeanne, I'm so sorry," and after a moment she let go of him and let me pull her away from the bed.

"He said he wouldn't, he promised he wouldn't," she gabbled, briefly resting her head on my shoulder before she tried to turn again, to return to Curtis. But she was weaker this time, so that I managed to turn her the other way, and she wrenched free of me and stumbled toward the hall. She was sobbing as she reached the bedroom door and turned back, one bloody hand on the door frame, to look again at her husband.

Curtis was lying on his back in the bed, his upper torso propped up with pillows, his blue eyes staring vacantly at the ceiling. He hadn't been dead long—how long I couldn't guess, but I could tell it hadn't been long; I'd have guessed it was under two hours. He'd been shot once, only once that I could see, and I had a hunch that might turn out to be important.

The room was stiflingly hot—of course, because the thermostat downstairs would have been cooled by the open window—so we wouldn't be able to get much information from body temperature.

Behind me, Jeanne ran for the bathroom at the top of the landing and started vomiting into the toilet.

I'd have stopped her if I'd had any idea how to do so. Very few law enforcement officers forget the case of Sam Sheppard, even as long ago and far away (from me, anyway) as it had happened: A doctor was accused of killing his wife. There was a lot of unexplained evidence, including a cigarette floating in an upstairs toilet. Nobody in the household smoked, and that cigarette was one piece of evidence pointing away from Sheppard. Today, we'd probably be able to get DNA evidence from the cigarette butt, but even that long ago there would have been about a 60 percent chance of getting the blood type from it, because about 60 percent of humanity, called "secretors," have saliva and tears that carry blood type information. But somebody working on the investigation flushed, and Sam Sheppard spent ten years in prison before being released on appeal. It wasn't until this year that DNA examination of some blood collected at the scene proved Sheppard innocent.

I didn't know whether there was a cigarette in Curtis and Jeanne's main upstairs toilet (and come to think of it, there were at least two more bathrooms upstairs, one off Jeanne's room and one off what I then thought was the guest bedroom). I hadn't had a chance to look before Jeanne got sick, and now any evidence that might have been there was hopelessly contaminated.

All of it happened in less time than it took me, just now, to think about it.

It had all happened so fast that Sue was barely up the stairs, had barely elbowed herself past me for a look at Curtis, before Jeanne had flushed, rinsed her mouth, and resumed weeping, a heavy, doleful sound in the quiet house. Then she started retching again, with nothing at all left in her stomach. "Sue, don't go in Curtis's room," I said, and then I took two steps toward Jeanne's room to use the telephone, to call dispatch to ask for an ambulance, because Jeanne was certainly going to need one and Sue might, and to ask for all the inevitable paraphernalia and personnel I work with every day.

But I didn't reach the telephone, because Sue of course did go in there or at least look in there, screamed "Nooo!", turned so hard and fast that she slammed her back against the wall behind me, and ran back down the stairs toward the half-bath off the laundry room, both hands over her mouth.

Terrific. Barfing in stereo. And it wasn't even a particularly gruesome scene. But on the other hand it wasn't *my* husband or brother.

Belatedly I shut the door to the room Curtis lay in. I didn't need to go inside again to see that he was dead; I'd seen that before I pulled Jeanne away from him. I started again to go into Jeanne's room to use the telephone, but I hadn't reached it before Sue screamed, "Deb!"

There was an overtone, an undertone, to her voice, and I dashed back down the stairs even faster than I had gone up them. "Where are you?" I called.

"In here."

I followed her voice to the laundry room, or rather, to the bathroom beside the laundry room. There was nothing I could see that would have prompted her to call me.

"Is he dead too?" she asked, her voice quavering, and finally I saw what she was looking at.

This house was elegant; like my Aunt Brume, Jeanne had the gift of elegance, but unlike my Aunt Brume, Jeanne had the ability to make elegance look comfortable. Even the laundry room was neatly arranged and tastefully painted, with one nice, small Georgia O'Keeffe flower print hanging beside the door. Even the little half-bath off the laundry room had an attractive peach-colored rug on the floor, and another, larger Georgia O'Keeffe on its very pale peach wall.

The dog sprawled in the middle of the rug did not go well with the elegance.

I knew Polka; he often, but not always, went jogging with us. Dalmatians are friendly, if bossy and disobedient, dogs, and whenever I was at Jeanne's house Polka came straight to me, demanding an appropriate greeting, scratching and sometimes pawing gently at my hand when I stopped petting him. I should have noticed that he didn't greet me this day, but of course I'd had too much else on my mind.

No, he wasn't dead. I could tell that, and Sue would have been able to tell also if she hadn't been too distraught to take a moment to watch him. His chest rose and fell gently. But he was definitely unconscious, lying on his side on the rumpled peach rug, and as I leaned over him I could see what was oddest: his collar was twisted.

He couldn't possibly have worn the collar like that for any length of time; it would have been miserable on him, and any person who saw it—particularly Jeanne, with her love for order—would have straightened it immediately.

The only possible explanation was that somebody must have taken the collar off him and then put it back on, probably in great haste, sometime later and after Polka was unconscious.

That didn't make a bit of sense.

But at least it seemed to have distracted Sue from wanting to vomit. I glanced at the toilet, but it had been flushed since its last use, and the towels were all fresh and crisp, still with slight creases where they had been folded. Nobody had used this bathroom since it was last cleaned.

I picked the dog up, rug and all, and carried him into the living room, setting him (still on the rug) on the pale blue couch and taking one of the abundant silk-covered cushions to put under his head to raise it a little bit from body level. As profoundly out as he was, I thought he might need a little help breathing, but I didn't feel ready to give mouth-to-mouth resuscitation to a dog. Anyway, dogs like to use pillows.

He whined a little but didn't wake when I lifted his head to scoot the cushion under it. And that too was odd: even when they're medicated dogs tend to be light sleepers. *At least some dogs do*, I thought ruefully; our accidentally acquired cocker spaniel Ivory has a tendency to lie on his back with all four feet in the air and snore. Waking him between midnight and six A.M. is a near-impossibility. Several times Harry has picked him up from the bed, carried him into the living room, and deposited him—still on his back—on the couch without Ivory ever awakening. This has had the annoying result of making Pat, our accidentally acquired pit bull, even more obnoxiously defensive: he seems to have decided it is now his duty to protect Ivory as well as the people.

But this was a Dalmatian, and they tend to be pretty alert dogs. Furthermore, it was full daylight, and, unlike cats, dogs are not even semi-nocturnal. Polka ought to be awake.

I went to the kitchen phone, then hesitated. Criminals have been known to use telephones in victims' houses, so it's best for police not to use a phone until after it has been tested for fingerprints.

But there were not very many alternatives. I didn't have a radio with me. I didn't have my car with me. Although Jeanne would be glad to lend me her car, I wasn't sure she was up to finding the keys right now. Although Sue would let me use the phone at her house two blocks away, I wasn't sure she was any more up to finding keys than Jeanne was. So the options boiled down to these: (1) I could go to a neighbor's house to use the phone, except that with husband and wife both working in about 90 percent of all households, my chances of finding anybody at home this time of day were slim (which, of course, is the reason residential burglaries are nearly all done in the daytime now). (2) I could go to Sue's house, which was nearby, but as I mentioned, that would once again require Sue to find her keys. (3) I could run home and use my own phone. Right, and my house was eight blocks away and I'd be leaving the crime scene unguarded and two women—one of them definitely hysterical and the other heading that way—unprotected and unsupervised for the time it took me *literally* to run eight blocks, make the phone call, and then return by car. (4) I could send Jeanne or Sue to telephone for help, except that both of them were shocky and certainly not up to running errands, at least not errands that demanded coherence, and besides that they'd have as much trouble finding someone at home as I would. Or (5) I could use the phone here.

I used the phone in the kitchen, it being the one I supposed (for no particular reason) that the killer had been least likely to use. I held it awkwardly by the mouthpiece and dialed by pushing the buttons with a wooden skewer, in hopes of not damaging evidence any more than I could avoid. The dispatcher had no trouble with my request for an ambulance, crime scene crew, medical examiner, and Captain Millner, but I had a little trouble convincing him I *really* had to have a veterinarian immediately. But he finally agreed to send for one of the small-animal doctors who advertised traveling clinics. Task one accomplished—and I didn't have a notebook with me, so I'd have to find some paper to start making notes. Well, that could wait a few minutes.

I called my husband, Harry, then, to tell him I'd be late getting home and not to worry. "I just had this hunch you were going to be late," he said, "in view of the fact that you're already late. So I already made breakfast, and we ate and I got Cameron dressed, and I'll be taking off in just a minute to get Cameron to kindergarten."

As our normal weekday breakfast is Cheerios, I did not feel that Harry's making it represented an unreasonable burden. And our five-year-old, Cameron, now dresses himself. Persuading him not to wear green pants with an orange shirt, or other such tasteful combinations, sometimes can take a little while, but Harry is as persuasive as I am in these matters.

Rather distractedly I told him what had happened, and he said, "Tell her I'm sorry to hear it. And look, don't worry about home, I'll take care of things here."

"Thanks," I said, and wondered *what* things. The only things left to do this morning were put away the milk and Cheerios, put the bowls and spoons into the sink, and lock Pat in the backyard, as the mail carrier refuses to deliver mail when Pat is in the front yard.

Sue had followed me into the living room with Polka, had followed me into the kitchen where I used the phone, and now stood staring at me as if I had some way of undoing what had been done. I asked her if she felt she could just sit down in the living room and let me go talk to Jeanne. She nodded, sat down on the couch beside Polka, and then said, "I guess I could make some coffee."

"I guess you could do that," I agreed.

She looked at me as if she'd never seen me before. "You don't drink coffee, do you?"

"No," I said, "but if you feel you and Jeanne need some—"

"I could make hot chocolate. That's what you drink. Or tea. Do you drink tea?"

"Don't worry about me," I said. "Just take care of yourself for now, okay?"

"Okay." She moved as if she were sleepwalking into the kitchen. I could hear the rattle of utensils, the sound of water running, as I went back upstairs.

"Jeanne?" I called.

"In here."

She was lying on her side on her bed, still in the cute pink plush jogging suit with the white Persian kitten appliqued on the shirt, her shoes still on and rubbing mud from Tuesday's rain onto her jacket, where her feet were resting, and her inadequately washed hands rubbing blood from Curtis's wound—not much of that, which was one of the things that told me he'd died fast—onto the duvet. Her eyes were wide open, staring at the wall, and except for their motion, and the occasional moaning sob, she would have looked as dead as her husband. But she turned, then, to look at me, and started speaking before I asked anything.

"He was talking about suicide at first, right after it happened," she said dully. "But then he stopped. He stopped even before he got out of the hospital. And when he got home he said he had to have his gun because somebody was trying to kill him. And he might've been right, because over the last couple of years some funny things have happened. So—and the doctor had him on antidepressants, and he had stopped talking about suicide—I thought maybe he really did need his gun. And I let him have it."

"How long ago was that?" I asked.

She hesitated. "I don't know," she said finally. "It's been a while. More than a year. Eighteen months or something like that, I guess. Maybe more than that. I gave it to him right after he got out of the hospital, but I can't remember how long ago that was. You'd think I would, wouldn't you, but there was just so much happening. And he'd have gotten it anyway, somehow, if I didn't give it to him, even if he had to pull himself all over the floor on his belly. He—Curtis always could get guns. Always could find guns. But he didn't—I mean, he'd stopped talking about suicide. I was trying to keep him feeling hopeful. And—there really are advances being made in this kind of thing. That foundation that actor guy set up, or is involved with, or something, you know, the one who fell off his horse, the one that played Superman, you know who I mean?"

She didn't wait for an answer. "They really are making advances. They've learned to fix spinal cords on rats, so they'll get to people soon. I kept telling him, we'll keep the physical therapist coming so his muscles wouldn't atrophy completely, and then someday he would be able to walk again because they're really making advances, you know, in treating spinal cord injury."

She paused, but I could tell she wasn't through talking yet. I just listened.

"I told him if he'd just wait—things would be better—and he kept telling me I didn't love him anymore, I might as well leave, there was plenty of money—Deb, I didn't *want* to leave! And who cares if there's plenty of money? Money doesn't keep you warm at night. He didn't want me to sleep with him—he said I wiggled around and kept him awake—but—"

She broke down into wild sobbing again, and I asked, deliberately briskly, "Could I call your pastor? Or priest—I don't know what church you go to."

"We don't go to church," she said dully. "I guess there's a God but I don't know one. Neither did Curtis."

"Family—"

She shook her head again. "Kenneth is at boarding school. And there's not anybody else."

I must have looked startled, because she glanced at me, half-smiling. "Our son. He's twelve. You've never met him. Curtis didn't want children. He said—hostages to fortune. You know. If you get kids you have to take care of them and that might cramp your style." She half-laughed, bitterly. "It sure would have cramped his. I did, often enough.

"So when I got pregnant he was mad and when I wouldn't get an abortion he was madder. But then when it turned out to be a boy, he got a little happy. He said it might be nice, have a son he could take fishing and camping and all that macho stuff." She half-chuckled again despite the sorrow in her eyes. "So wouldn't you know it, Kenneth came out my build—short and thin. And on top of that he's nearsighted and he has a lot of allergies. Curtis—Curtis wasn't pleased." She wiped her eyes, blew her nose, and resumed sobbing for a moment before adding, "Curtis wanted him to be in boarding school because he—Kenneth—was in Curtis's way. I wanted him in boarding school because that way he was safe from Curtis's temper. And don't doubt that even in a wheelchair he could do damage. Physically as well as emotionally."

I didn't doubt it. I must have been looking appalled, because she said, "I guess you think I should have left Curtis. Well, maybe I should have, for Kenneth's sake. But I've always felt like—you get married, you get married for life. And anyway I did love Curtis. He was nice to me . . . most of the time . . . So—no. I'll have to let Kenneth know, of course. But—I don't think there'll be any mourning there. And I don't want Kenneth brought home to comfort me. Other family—no. There's just not any. For Curtis or me either one."

"I could call your doctor," I offered.

She sat up shakily. "Poor Deb! You do this for a living, don't you? And you're going down the checklist, things to say to the widow?"

"Yes," I said, "but you know I really care."

"Deb, you'd really care if a cat was bereaved. No, I know you care. I know you do. But what good would any of it do? The doctor's not going to make Curtis alive again, an army of doctors couldn't, or an army of preachers. He's dead—"

She started weeping again, the temporary bravado evaporating quickly.

I asked, "Do you have any Valium? Or Xanax, anything like that?"

Through her sobbing, she said, "Curtis—I think in his bathroom—I don't want it now but maybe I'll take it later."

On the way to Curtis's bathroom, which was the main bathroom at the top of the stairs and was accessible from both the landing and Curtis's bedroom, I took a few extra seconds to have a good look at the corpse.

Somebody might have wanted it to look like suicide. If so, the person didn't know Curtis very well and didn't know crime scenes very well.

The pistol, a 9 mm semiautomatic, was lying on the floor

beneath his right hand, which draped off the side of the bed.

The entry wound was in his left forehead, and from the looks of it, the pistol had been fired from directly in front of his head, though how far away I wasn't prepared to guess except that it wasn't within a foot.

I knew that, because there was no powder tattooing around it.

And Curtis, as I knew very well, was left-handed. So he might have shot himself in the left side of the forehead, but he couldn't do it with the pistol more than a foot away, and he wouldn't have then dropped the pistol on the right side of the bed.

Curtis's bathroom looked just as I would expect any bathroom in Jeanne's care to look—clean, elegant—except that it was well arranged for a paraplegic; Jeanne must have had the room remodeled before he got out of the hospital. A high toilet with grab bars, so that a man could move himself from a wheelchair to it. A shower arranged so that a wheelchair would fit into it. Low towel bars, low storage for things like toilet paper and extra towels. And a medicine cabinet low enough for a man in a wheelchair to reach it.

For years pharmacists have been warning that the bathroom, with its heat and humidity, is the absolutely worst place in the house to store medication. I am always amazed to find out how many people store it there anyway. Curtis, or Jeanne, or one of Curtis's nurses, kept it there.

Quite a little array it was. Antibiotics. Prozac. Naproxyn. Tylenol Three. Flexeril. And, yes, Valium.

It is a violation of federal law to give prescription medicine prescribed for one person to another person. I suspect that is a law that is frequently violated, just as it was going to be violated right now. I shook two five-milligram Valium tablets into my hand, got a paper cup full of water, and headed for Jeanne's room.

No, I wasn't going to administer it myself; the EMTs would do that as soon as they came with the ambulance.

Before I got there, I heard noises from downstairs. "Sue, what is it?" I yelled.

"It's an ambulance driver," Sue yelled back. "What do you want him to do?"

"I'll be there in just a second." I went downstairs, went out on the front steps with the EMT to talk with him briefly, and then watched while he checked Sue's blood pressure.

"You want to go to the hospital?" he asked her.

"No, what would I want to do that for?"

He shook his head at me. "She's okay," he said. "Anything else?"

I took him upstairs to Jeanne, and he checked her blood pressure. "Ma'am," he said, "I really think we ought to take you to the hospital for a few minutes and let a doctor have a look at you."

"Well, I'm not going," she said.

He looked at me. As I could have predicted, he asked, "Do you know if there's any Valium in the house? Or Xanax, anything like that?"

I gestured toward the end table, the two yellow tablets. "That's good," he said. "If you'll just take these, ma'am—"

"I'm not going to do that, either," she said. "At least not now. I need to be awake to help the police. I'll take them later. I'm fine, though. Really I am."

He shook his head, got out a form labeled "Patient refused transport," and had me sign as a witness. Then he departed.

Before he was all the way down the stairs, Sue called, "Deb, there's somebody else here."

"Who?" I asked.

"Gerry's here. Gerry Scamander."

"Who's she?"

"He. He's Curtis's daytime nurse. What do you want me to do?"

"Keep him there," I said. "I'll be down in a minute."

# 2

SUE WAS UPSTAIRS SITTING WITH JEANNE. Before sending her there—for that matter, before going downstairs at all—I had checked the remaining upstairs bathrooms, the one attached to Jeanne's room and the one attached to what I had thought was a guest room but had now learned was Kenneth's room for the rare occasions when he was at his so-called home, and when I got downstairs I checked the other two downstairs bathrooms. (*A six-bathroom house for three people, one of whom is rarely present—egads!* I thought, having grown up as one of six children and two adults in a one-bathroom house.) Of course I had already looked at the half-bath before removing Polka from it. I couldn't see anything in any of them that didn't look as if it belonged there. Not that I had really expected to see anything. As Curtis had not been shot at close range, there was no reason why his killer should have needed to clean up after the killing.

I was wondering now about that window Jeanne had found open. But before I checked it, I needed to have a little talk with Gerry Scamander.

Liberating some index cards and a ball-point pen from the drawer of the telephone table, I sat down in a chair opposite him and took a good look at him. I'd guess him as being in his early twenties, with tousled light-brown hair, pale blue eyes, and bitten fingernails. He wasn't very tall, and he wasn't very heavy. He wasn't very short, and he wasn't very thin. He was about as ordinary-looking a person as I had seen in a long time.

He looked very nervous.

I could understand why a private nurse just informed his patient had been murdered might look very nervous. If I'd been him, I would have been wondering why Curtis was killed and whether I had inadvertently learned something, or somebody might think I had inadvertently learned something, that would send the killer after me next.

"Did Sue tell you anything?" I asked.

"Just that Curtis had shot himself." His voice was an unexpectedly deep baritone. And I was surprised to learn that Sue, at least, hadn't realized this was murder. But come to think of it, Jeanne hadn't either. I tend to forget that such things are not as obvious to other people as they are to me.

I would have liked to let the discussion go on with Gerry under that assumption, but I couldn't. I didn't know who was a suspect and who was not, which meant I had to treat everybody as a suspect.

"That's not exactly what happened," I said.

Gerry leaned back on the couch, his hand moving toward Polka. "Good. I didn't see how it could."

"Don't touch the dog," I said sharply.

"Huh? Why?" But he moved his hand back. "I already petted the dog," he added. "Why shouldn't I?"

"Possible evidence," I said. "Did you touch the collar?"

"No, why would I want to do that? He sure is out of it, isn't he?"

"Out of it?"

"You know. Asleep. Dozocious." He put both hands briefly up by the right side of his face and pantomimed sleep.

"Yeah," I said. "Back to what you were saying. You don't see how what could possibly—never mind. I'll get to that later. Let's get on to something else. Your name is Gerry Scamander? How do you spell that?"

"Which one?" he asked, in what seemed suspiciously like cool humor. "Gerry is G-E-R-R-Y. Short for Gerald. Scamander is just like it sounds." But he spelled it anyway, and then provided his address and telephone number, his age—twenty-five—and the school where he had gotten his nursing degree, which happened to be Texas Woman's University. "And no, I'm not gay," he added. "What good would it do a gay guy to have all those women around? But people always ask. It's just that TWU was close and convenient."

My one semester of college had been spent at TWU, and although I knew that court decisions had made it necessary to admit men a good many years ago, I remain puzzled as to why a man would *want* to go there.

I didn't ask. That was not the topic of my investigation.

Unfortunately, I also could not, right then at any rate, ask about anything that *was* the topic of my investigation. Having neither my car nor a police car with me had created numerous difficulties, some of them larger than others.

"Will you stay here," I said, "while I take a walk around the house?"

"Okay. Do you want me to answer the phone if it rings?"

"No," I said, and called upstairs, "Sue, if the phone rings, just let it ring."

Her assent was muffled with tears, and she might or might not remember; she might or might not have really even heard me, despite her answer. If she didn't it was probably no big deal; I had no reason to believe that the killer had ever used the phones anyway.

I went out the front door—it and the door frame both were solid steel, with a good deadbolt lock, but I knew already that the varnished natural wood on the outside and inside of the door was only a thick veneer—and turned left, on the lawn rather than the sidewalk. I quickly arrived at a six-foot-high cyclone fence that ran like the lower leg of a T from the side of the house to the property line, where it met another six-foot-high cyclone fence that ran both ways like the crossbar of the T. The fence had a row of barbed wire at the top, along with signs at intervals of about a yard and a half warning "Caution! Electrically charged fence!"

Although the ident tech, on arrival, would do a complete crime scene sketch, I decided to make a rough one of my own, without bothering with measurements, to keep things straight in my mind.

I sat down on the grass, which wasn't too soggy, all things considered, and made a sketch that stretched over several of the index cards. Then I stuck it all in my pocket, realizing that the grass had been soggier than I had thought and that my backside was now damp and cold, and resumed examining the yard.

The thick St. Augustine grass, with its broad, deep green leaves, showed no visible trace of Tuesday's rain, barely showed the beginning of fall. It did not show that anybody had gone over the fence. It probably would not show that anybody had gone over the fence unless they had pole-vaulted, leaving a hole in the lawn, or had been snagged so badly that they left some clothing and, maybe, some skin on the top of the fence.

But just inside the fence was a pyracantha hedge that looked about four feet wide, and pyracantha—fire-thorn, with deep green leaves in summer and bright red berries in winter—has worse thorns than mesquite. I could not make myself believe that anybody had climbed that fence and risked trying to jump from the top of it over the pyracantha, and I didn't really believe anybody was likely to have pole-vaulted, which might or might not have made clearing the hedge possible.

At the property line, the pyracantha paralleled the inside of the other fence, to create a dense hedge that extended clear out to the sidewalk and clear back to the line of pyracantha inside the back fence.

Interesting . . . most people find a four-foot-high fence, even by itself without an electric charge and a thorny hedge, quite adequate. Maybe Curtis really did think somebody was trying to kill him.

A tall cedar tree stood about three feet from the southeast corner of the house; its width and breadth was such that it

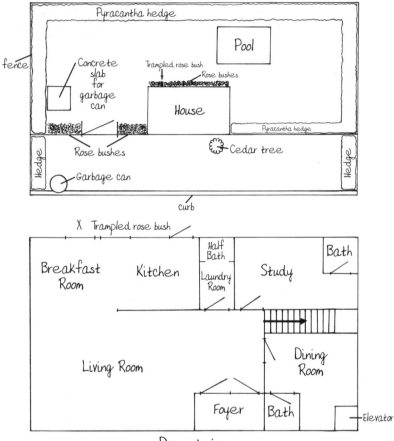

Pyracantha hedge

fence

Concrete slab for garbage can

Trampled rose bush

Rose bushes

Pool

House

Pyracantha hedge

Rose bushes

Cedar tree

Hedge

Hedge

Garbage can

curb

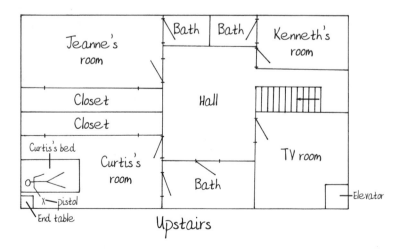

X  Trampled rose bush

Breakfast Room

Kitchen

Half Bath

Laundry Room

Study

Bath

Living Room

Dining Room

Foyer

Bath

Elevator

**Downstairs**

Jeanne's room

Bath

Bath

Kenneth's room

Closet

Closet

Hall

Curtis's bed

Curtis's room

Bath

TV room

X—pistol

End table

Elevator

**Upstairs**

effectively shielded the dining room window, making it impossible to see from the street.

Returning to the front door, I went right this time, around the house to the little scrap of fence, also pyracantha-guarded, on that side beside the gate to the backyard.

The gate was not just unlocked.

The charged wire that normally crossed it had been disconnected by the opening of the gate; I assumed from the warning signs which bristled on it that unless the security alarm system was on standby when the gate was opened, its opening would set off the alarm.

And on top of that it was open, with the expensive case-hardened padlock hanging open from the hasp where Jeanne must have left it because—

Of course.

Because it was trash pick-up day.

From where I was standing I could see the concrete slab where the trash can normally sat; I knew that was its usual location because I'd been in this backyard before, had swum in the heated swimming pool, which now had a metal frame around it that would hold a heavy plastic domed cover so that Jeanne could swim all winter; though of course when the pool and the frame were built, the important thing was that Curtis would be able to swim all winter.

I had appreciated Jeanne's invitation to swim whenever I wanted, though I'd taken her up on it only once. And then, because I wasn't looking for a way a killer could get in, the pyracantha hadn't fully registered on my mind.

The trash can was sitting on the curb. Jeanne must have hauled it out before we went jogging.

So often evidence is found in trash cans, where the criminal found it convenient to discard things on his line of departure. I sprinted over and gingerly opened the top.

I need not have been so careful. It was empty. The trash, along with any evidence that might have been inside, had already been taken away.

So, reconstruct. Jeanne got up early because I needed to go jogging early. She put the trash can out on the curb so it could be picked up; she put it out early because here, obviously, trash pickup is early. She intended to put it back on its concrete slab as soon as she got home, and then, of course, she'd have relocked the gate.

Somebody must have been watching the house, somebody must have known she went jogging on Thursday morning, must have known she'd leave the gate open until she could put the trash can back.

But who knew she was leaving early? That schedule change was at my request; probably if she'd left at her usual time the trash would already have been picked up, the can would already be in the backyard, the gate would already be relocked.

I knew. Sue knew. Jeanne knew.

Nobody else except, of course, my husband, and Sue's husband, who was usually out of town this part of the week, and Jeanne's husband, who now was dead. Nobody else at all, not unless Curtis really had been in as much danger as Jeanne thought he thought he was, not unless somebody had the phone tapped.

I stood indecisively at the gate for a moment longer; then I stepped through it, to see that the dense pyracantha hedge lined the entire inside of the backyard fence, totally surrounding the backyard except for the single gate and the back wall of the house—and the backyard was huge, so huge that there was plenty of grass, plenty of flower beds, despite the presence of the swimming pool and the hedge. In all, this house must have had more than four thousand square feet just of pyracantha, more formidable than a moat, unless the moat was full of piranhas.

Four thousand square feet of pyracantha, and an open gate. An open gate that Jeanne would probably never forgive herself for.

There was no pyracantha under the windows. Jeanne, or

Curtis, hadn't exactly fallen down on security—in addition to an electronic security system so good it made ours look like a child's toy, there were dozens of rosebushes, all bristling with thorns—but rosebushes are easier to fight with than pyracantha.

Directly under a window into the breakfast room, which was technically part of the kitchen, somebody had stepped hard on a rosebush, bending it to the ground and breaking its stem.

There was no usable footprint because Jeanne, or her gardener, had begun to prepare the roses for winter, and since the ground never actually freezes for more than a few days at a time here in Fort Worth, that involved heavy mulching. Beneath all the rosebushes was shredded hay, built up several feet, and at the east end of the rose bed shredded hay was piled up to completely cover the first two bushes. More bales of hay were sitting in the yard, presumably intended to be shredded and used to cover the rest of the bushes.

Somebody—the somebody who trod down the rosebush— had taken a bale of hay and set it under the window, between the trodden-down rosebush and the back wall of the house.

I'd found the means of entry; this was the window that Jeanne had slammed when we first arrived. The one she didn't remember opening.

The one she didn't remember opening because she didn't open it?

So who did?

And how had that person gotten around the electronic system? Because I *did* know it had been on; the little yellow light that went out only after Jeanne punched in the code told me that.

The kitchen door was locked; I checked.

Then I went back through the gate, into the front yard, where Captain Millner had just driven up.

# 3

Is THIS THE FACE THAT LAUNCHED A thousand ships, and burnt the topless towers of Ilium?" Captain Millner proclaimed, swinging his arms out widely.

That made no sense at all to me. Obviously it did to Gerry Scamander, who said "No" briefly and sourly.

"The Scamander is the river that flows past Troy," Millner explained to me.

"Oh," I said, for want of anything better to say. Then I returned to what I was doing, namely talking to Scamander. "I don't consider you a suspect," I said, as patiently as I could in view of the fact that I had already said it three times. "I don't consider *anybody* a suspect right now, but I'm going to have to ask Jeanne and Sue to sign the same forms even though they were both with me when the murder probably took place. The problem is that I don't know who is a possible suspect, and I don't want to ask anybody any questions unless I'm sure they understand their legal rights."

"Is this going to get me in trouble?" Scamander asked for the third time. "I remember on TV, that guy that first they said he set the Olympics bomb and then they said he didn't, the FBI tried to trick him into signing a rights waiver."

"I don't know what happened on that case," I said. "I didn't work it, and frankly I think it was badly worked. All I can tell you is that I'm not trying to trick you. I want to talk to you. But I want you to know you don't have to talk to me."

"Well, I know that. But—" He paused.

Beside me, Captain Millner—who had brought in the Miranda forms along with a lot of other paperwork—stirred uneasily. "If you don't want to sign it you don't have to," he said for the second time. "If you want to call a lawyer you can call a lawyer. If you don't want to talk to us you don't have to talk to us. Nobody is forced to talk to the police. It's that simple."

"Yeah, so I don't talk to you and then you arrest me or tell the press so everybody follows me around for the next hundred years."

"Curtis Minot is not that important a victim," I said softly. "No, we won't arrest you and we won't tell the press, but we might subpoena you and ask you questions in court, where you do have to answer anything that's not likely to be self-incriminating."

In fact, we probably wouldn't—lawyers try very hard to avoid asking any question in court to which they do not already know the answers—but we *might,* and so I saw a need to say so.

"Thing is," Scamander said, "I don't really know anything about this."

"Okay," I said.

"Thing is, I don't think he'd do it himself, but—"

"Okay," I said into the silence. He was about as hung up on "thing is" as Jeanne was on "I mean."

"You really just want to ask me questions?"

"That's right."

He looked indecisive a moment longer, then picked up the pen and signed. Captain Millner witnessed his signature quickly before he could change his mind again—although, of course, if he did change his mind at any point, we had to stop questioning him right then and there.

# 4

So I DON'T KNOW," SCAMANDER SAID, leaning back and petting the still-sleeping dog, from whom I (in the presence of Captain Millner) had removed the twisted collar, awkwardly because I didn't want to touch any of the metal, which might possibly hold prints. "I mean, sure, you've got to keep suicide in mind any time you're working with a paraplegic, because it's a horrible way to have to live, but he didn't do anything special to make me think he wanted to do it. He did say he had enemies."

"When did he say that?" I asked.

"Oh, he said that a lot of times."

"Did he ever give any names?"

"No."

"Did you ever meet any of those enemies?"

Scamander hesitated, and then said, "He spent about two hours quarreling on the phone a couple of days ago with some guy named Ellis, but after he hung up he told me this Ellis guy was his partner and there wasn't any real problem."

"What were they talking about?" I asked.

"I couldn't tell. They weren't making much sense. And the words Curtis was using—it was like they were talking in some kind of code."

Captain Millner caught my eye and signaled for me to leave that line of questioning. Obviously there was something else he wanted to find out about before we followed that path.

Without really noticing anything had changed, Scamander

went on cheerfully talking. "And, let me see, yeah, there was this one other guy."

"What one other guy?"

"I don't remember his whole name. Curtis called him Bran. You know, like cereal, only he pronounced it a little different. Bran called a couple of times and then he came here to the house, and he was about as mad as an old wet hen. He was as mad as I've ever seen anybody."

"What about, could you tell?"

"It was something about guns," Scamander said. "They were rusty. This guy had bought a whole lot of guns from Curtis and about half of them were too rusty to use. And he was really mad. Curtis gave him back some of his money, but that didn't get him any less mad. The last thing he said before he left was, he said, 'I'd kill you, but you aren't worth the powder and shot it would take to blow you to somewhere where there ain't no snow.' And Curtis just laughed. Come to think of it, that was one of the things Curtis was talking about on the phone when he was talking to that guy Ellis."

Captain Millner and I looked at each other again; then I asked, "Can you tell us any more? About this Bran and about the transaction? Do you think Bran was from some sort of militia group?" Like me, Captain Millner was probably having trouble thinking of anybody who would need to buy a lot of guns sight unseen.

"No, that's all I know," Scamander said, "except Bran, he had some sort of a foreign accent. Like he was Australian or something. Maybe English. Or Scottish, that might be it."

"Or Irish?" Millner asked softly, making the same mental leap I had just made myself.

"Yeah, maybe Irish," Scamander said. "What makes you think that?"

"Guns," Millner said. "A whole lot of guns. They aren't often smuggled into Australia. They are often smuggled into Ireland."

"Well, sure," Scamander said. "I should have thought of

that. Guns, sure. Into Ireland. And bombs too, except Curtis didn't have any bombs, or at least if he did I didn't ever hear about it. And when Curtis opened that safe in his study to give that Bran guy that money, man, I've never seen so much money in my life. And after he—Bran, I mean—left, I said gun-running must be good business, and Curtis, he said, yeah, if you went at it right." Scamander looked up, looked at me, looked at Millner. "You did know he was a gunrunner, didn't you?"

# III

THURSDAY, NOVEMBER 11

# 1

No, OF COURSE I DIDN'T KNOW HE WAS a gunrunner, not until Scamander started talking about guns," I said crossly to Captain Millner. "And even then I didn't know he was running them himself. He could just as easily have been technically legal and been selling guns under the table to the real runner. Anyway, why should I have known? I was told he was a retired businessman, and I never talked business with him. How much do you know about the wives of the men you play handball with?"

Captain Millner's addiction to handball might have been one of the reasons why he, at sixty-eight, was still chief of detectives and showed no signs of slowing down on anything. Eventually the city would make him retire, but he didn't intend to leave one second before he had to.

"Touché," he said thoughtfully. "Most of them I don't even know by sight."

"Anyway, I *still* don't know."

We were sitting out in front of the house in his unmarked police car, that being the only place we could talk and be reasonably certain of not being overheard. I felt guilty about not being with Jeanne, but if I had been with Jeanne I would have felt guilty about not being busy trying to find out who had killed her husband.

"What do you mean, you still don't know?" Millner asked now.

"We have Gerry Scamander's word for it," I said. "Nobody

else's. Scamander looks to me like the kind of person who would embroider a story to make it prettier. And I *know* Curtis was that kind of person; I've heard him embroidering, and known what he was doing because Jeanne had already told me the same story without embroidery. So either one—or, for that matter, both—of them could have exaggerated. Or out-and-out lied."

"Do you think you can get her to sign a consent search?"

*Her*, obviously, meant Jeanne. "I probably can," I said, "but I'm not sure whether it would hold up in court."

"How so? Grieving widow and all that?"

"Grieving widow that the EMTs and I gave ten milligrams of Valium to an hour or so ago. She didn't take it then, though, so she might still not have taken it. I'll go and check."

"While you're doing that," he said, "I'm going to find out whether Minot had a federal firearms license." He opened the car door and leaned forward, about to get out.

"Before you start using the telephone," I said, "you better give me a consent search form."

"Oh, that's right, you walked here. Kind of careless, wasn't it? I'll bet you don't even have your pistol on you."

"I *ran* here. And no, I don't have my pistol on me. I rarely go jogging armed or carrying a briefcase, and I wasn't expecting a murder. Look, you're the one who was having a fit about my physical fitness or lack thereof."

"One of," he said mildly. "I wasn't the only one. My briefcase is inside the house. Come on; I'll get you that and some other paperwork. Aren't we glad I carry extra?"

I decided not to dignify that remark with a reply.

# 2

JEANNE WAS LYING ON HER SIDE, HER FACE toward the window overlooking the backyard, and Sue had gone into the guest room—Kenneth's room, I reminded myself again—and was also lying down. I couldn't resist thinking of Emily Dickinson's lines:

> The Bustle in a House
> The Morning after Death
> Is Solemnest of industries
> Enacted upon earth—
>
> The Sweeping up the Heart
> And putting Love away
> We shall not want to use again
> Until Eternity.

Of course, this was actually the morning *of* death rather than the morning *after* death, but the only bustle in this house right now came from police officers. Irene Loukas, head of the identification section, had taken this call herself, with Bob Castle to assist her. The first thing she had done on arrival was check for fingerprints on all the telephones, so they would be available for use, and then start on the doors and door frames, while Bob investigated outside more thoroughly than I had done in my brief survey. I had told him about the open window and the crushed rosebush, and he had taken photographs preparatory to removing the hay and leaning a ladder up against the wall to look for trace evidence—hair, fibers, or anything else that might have rubbed off the killer's clothes and caught on brick or mortar—and then dust for fingerprints.

Irene was extremely annoyed with me for leaving my fingerprints so many places, so that when she got back into the office she'd have to pull out my fingerprint card and eliminate them, but what was I supposed to do? When I got here I had no reason to think this house was soon to be treated as a crime scene, and when I did know it was a crime scene there were still things I had to do. Anyway, I was a frequent visitor to this house, and it was inevitable that my prints would linger here and there.

There had been, she told me, no fingerprints on any of the phones. And that rather interested her as well as me.

Usually there are no usable fingerprints on a telephone, because so many people use a phone, holding it the same way, that what's left has all the coherence of a bowl of spaghetti.

But finding no prints at all on a telephone, especially on several telephones in the same house, was distinctly intriguing.

Assistant medical examiner Andrew Habib, M.D., drove up with Richard Olsen, one of his investigators, just as I was about to go up the stairs; I heard the patrol officer at the front door—one Andrew Jackson, whom I had not previously met, he being a product of the most recent recruit school—asking who they were. Their arrival delayed my next talk with Jeanne a little more, but such a delay shouldn't matter unless she hadn't taken the Valium yet and decided to do so before I got there. I couldn't see that happening. If she was like family members of most murder victims, she was so far into shock that she wouldn't do anything for a while unless somebody told her to do it.

I had been in and out of the death room a couple of times, but I'd tried to avoid the immediate crime area. Now, Irene and I crowded in behind Habib and Olsen. "Yep, I would say he is most thoroughly defunct," Habib said cheerfully and loudly, and looked at his watch. His report would include the exact time at which Curtis was pronounced dead.

"His wife is in the next room," I told him in an undertone, and he looked slightly startled.

"Sorry," he said, and then added, "Man, it's hot in here." He shed his jacket and handed it behind him, not even looking to see who would take it and put it outside the room. (I was the one who did; then I closed the bedroom door and hoped that the storage closets between the two rooms would sufficiently muffle anything else that was said in here. Habib's *joie de vivre* tends to be somewhat irrepressible.) "How come it's so hot?" he asked me.

"It's so hot," I said, "because there was a window open downstairs near the thermostat."

Habib glanced around at me. "Are you sure?" he said.

"Of course I'm sure. I was here when it was closed."

"What can you tell me about this case?" he asked, and I told him. He *hmm*ed thoughtfully a few times—this one of his habits I detest—and then said, "So he was paraplegic."

"Yes."

"How long, do you know?"

"A couple of years."

"Paraplegics get chilled pretty easily. Not as bad as quadriplegics, of course, but bad enough. Mightn't they have kept the room this warm deliberately?"

"Definitely not," I said. "Look, I told you, I know these people."

"Well, it sure as heck wasn't suicide."

"I'd already decided that," I said, "but why have you decided so fast?"

"Cadaveric spasm."

"Oh really! I didn't notice that."

Cadaveric spasm, a sort of postmortem rigidity, is not the same thing as rigor mortis, which arrives gradually, starting and ending in the chest and jaw. Normally rigor mortis takes anywhere from six to twenty or so hours—depending on a lot of independent variables including ambient temperature, cause of death, and size and previous physical condition of the decedent—to be complete. Cadaveric spasm occurs only in absolutely instant death. It stiffens the body as much as rigor mortis does, which might be a little confusing except for one thing: Under normal circumstances a body becomes completely limp after death; the muscles all relax. The eyes are half-open, the jaw is slack, the hands are half-open, and anything the victim might have been holding drops free. Then, as rigor mortis phases in, the body essentially freezes in the formerly relaxed position.

Whoever put the pistol beneath his outstretched right hand probably knew that.

But in cadaveric spasm, every muscle instantly goes into a tensed state, and anything that was in the hand stays there. I'd once worked a suicide in which it took five people to pry a pistol out of the hand of a ninety-five pound woman (five people using considerable caution, as the semiautomatic she'd used might easily go off again from her continuing pressure on the trigger).

It was too early for rigor mortis to have begun, so if this body was stiff it was stiff because of cadaveric spasm. And in that case, if he'd shot himself the pistol would still be in his hand.

Which it was not.

Not that that told me anything I wasn't already sure of, but it should clench the case against suicide adequately for even the most skeptical of jurors.

As I had followed this train of thought, Habib had resumed his *hmm*ing, gotten out a scalpel, and nicked a slight slit in Curtis's—the victim's; if I had to work this case, and Captain Millner had already told me I did, then I had to depersonalize the victim in order to be able to think objectively—abdomen to insert a thermometer into the liver, and *hmm*ed some more. "I guess you want time of death," he asked over his shoulder.

"You guess right."

"What kind of terminus do you have?"

"I don't know," I said.

He looked around at me again, a rather annoyed expression on his face. "Why don't you? You were jogging with his wife; you ought to know—"

"Well, I'm sorry, I don't know. I already told you what time I got here, and he was dead then, and had been dead long enough the blood was sticky. I know about what time his wife left the house, namely about six-fifteen, because I know what time I was supposed to meet her, which was six-thirty, and she was there on time. She always is; she's a prompt sort of person. What I don't know is whether she looked into this room before she left the house. She might have. She might not. I don't know."

"Then would you please go and ask."

Normally Habib is one of the most cheerful people I know; the sarcastic bite in his voice was distinctly unusual, and I wondered what was going on. But I didn't ask him. Meekly, I went to talk with Jeanne. I had to do that anyway.

I practically tiptoed into her room and then thought how silly I was being, the way all children, when they reach a certain age, sort of but not completely understand not to disturb their mother when she's asleep unless there's an emergency. They then decide that whispering "Hey, Mom" in her ear until she wakes up does not constitute disturbing her. So why was I walking quietly when I had to wake Jeanne anyway?

It didn't matter. As soon as I opened her door she turned over and looked at me.

And her signature would be valid. The two Valium tablets were still lying on the bedside table, along with the paper cup of water.

"I'm sorry," I said, "but I need to ask you a few questions. Is now okay?"

"It might as well be. But why? I mean, if he shot himself—" Tears began to well into her eyes again, and she dashed them away angrily with the back of her hand.

"Jeanne, he didn't shoot himself."

She sat up, grabbed a tissue, wiped her face with it. "What do you mean? I saw—"

"You saw him dead. You saw a gun nearby. That doesn't make it suicide. It was murder disguised to look like suicide—and frankly, it wasn't disguised very well."

"Then it's my fault," she said, tears dripping quietly down her face.

"No it isn't. It's the fault of whoever did it."

"Not if I let them in the house."

"Did you?"

"Not deliberately. But—" She started shaking her head and momentarily forgot to stop. Then she grabbed another tissue and wiped her face.

She blew her nose, loudly, dropped the tissue into the small pink wicker trash can beside her bed, grabbed another, blew her nose again, and said, "Sorry. Ladylike crying never was my forte."

"Why should it be?"

"Good ol' Deb," she said. "You're so realistic."

I wasn't sure whether that was a compliment or not, and I was distinctly surprised, considering how many people keep telling me I'm completely unrealistic or, like my daughters, telling me I'm funny.

"Okay, what do you need to ask?" She sat up on the bed, crossing her legs (still with her muddy shoes on, in complete disregard of the beautiful, expensive silk satin duvet). "I'll be sensible for a while. I'll be very sensible. As long as you don't expect too much. And you won't." She looked at me expectantly.

Tired of standing, I grabbed the chair from the dressing table, pulled it over by the bed, and sat down on it. "The medical examiner wants to know whether you looked in on Curtis before you left this morning."

She hesitated a minute. "No, I didn't," she said finally. "Why?"

"We're just trying to figure out as close as possible to an exact time of death."

"Can't they tell that from—from the body?"

"No," I said, "not within several hours. That's why we look for things aside from the body condition that would give us an earliest possible time and a latest possible time. If you'd looked in early this morning, then you could tell us he was alive when you left the house. You did mention he was still asleep."

"That's because the first thing he does when he wakes up is start yelling for me. And he hadn't. I thought about waking him to tell him I was going out early, but then I decided not to because I did tell him yesterday, and he'd been up pretty late last night, listening to a radio talk show, and I figured he'd probably sleep till I got back." She grabbed for another tissue and then, for the first time, seemed to notice the mud.

"So last time you saw him alive was—?"

"A little after midnight." She was now taking off her shoes and dropping each one, with a slight thud, into the lined wastebasket beside her bed. "I looked in to see if he wanted me to take him to the bathroom and he told me to hush, he was listening to Art Bell. That's a radio talk show. So I went on to bed. He doesn't listen to Art Bell all the time, but when he does he sits up about three quarters of the night. I think it's on till about four in the morning."

"Oh, yes," I agreed. "Harry sometimes listens to Art Bell. I don't have the time to waste."

She chuckled slightly, as her socks, which were not muddy, followed her shoes into the trash. "I'm afraid to. It seems to be addictive. But anyway, that was the last time I saw him— alive"—she turned her head away from me, swallowed, and turned back toward me—"and I didn't check on him this morning. I didn't have any reason to. I just got up about five-thirty, dressed and took out the trash, got a slice of toast and a cup of coffee—I told you about opening the window and triggering the alarm, and it had started going off before I got to the box to turn it off, and I figured that would wake Curtis up, but it didn't, or at least he didn't let me know if it did and I think he would have. Then I had the toast and coffee, and then I went over to Sue's for us to go together to meet you. I didn't shower first because I knew I'd need a shower when I got back. And before you ask, no, I didn't hear a pistol shot during the night. I might sleep soundly, but not soundly enough to miss something like that. And I'd certainly have heard one after I was up, even when I was in the backyard." The jacket, which was now muddy from her lying on it with muddy shoes, went into the wastebasket.

"Okay," I said, "I'm going to go tell Habib that, and then I've got to go downstairs to get some paperwork. There are some things we need you to sign."

"What about?" She was now taking off her watch and putting it neatly into the drawer of her bedside table.

"Oh, giving us permission to do a complete crime scene search, that kind of thing. I'll explain them when I give them to you. I poked around a little outside already, but not much."

"Outside?" Her face, reappearing from the depths of the sweatshirt she was pulling off over her head, paled suddenly, even more than its normal old-ivory pallor. "The gate where I took the trash out. I left it open. That's what I meant about my fault—if I left the gate open, and I did—did he—the person—whoever shot Curtis—come in through it? Was that how he got in the house, through that gate and then in that window I left open? Because if that window *was* open when I reset the alarm, then going through it wouldn't—" She paused, tossing her sweatpants on top of the sweatshirt into the trash, and then said, "Wouldn't set it off. And if it was closed it would set it off. I mean, it would if somebody tried to open it. Because I did reset the alarm before I left." In white bra and panties, she sat back down on the bed, carefully avoiding the mud and the blood.

"Maybe," I said. "I don't know yet, and neither does anybody else. As to the window, you said yourself that wasn't the one you opened."

I didn't have to guess what she was thinking, though I would have anyway, as her hands balled into fists in her lap and she muttered, "But I might have forgotten. It might have been. I mean—if it wasn't, how did anybody get the window open without triggering the alarm? So I had to have left it open. And the gate—so *stupid* of me."

"Jeanne, don't punish yourself. You didn't do anything stupid. As far as the window is concerned, I think you opened the one you thought you opened. There are always people who can get around security systems, if they know what they're doing. And don't you always leave the gate open until you get the trash can back on its slab?"

She looked at me. "Yes," she said, "but that doesn't mean it isn't a stupid thing to do. When I *know* Curtis thinks—thought his life was being threatened. And anyway I'm usually home."

"But did you really believe that his life was in danger? Did you have any reason to believe him?"

She sat still for a moment, then shook her head. "No. Not really. I mean—there's this saying, speak only good of the dead—I think that's some sort of superstition. You don't say anything bad about somebody dead because if you do they might come back and haunt you. Well, I don't think Curtis is going to come back and haunt me. I was married to him twenty-five years. And you don't have to be around him much more than twenty-five minutes to know he kind of stretches—stretched—the truth. I mean—you knew it, didn't you?"

"I'm afraid I did." As I'd noticed before, she was having a bad attack of the *I means*.

She swung her feet over to the edge of the bed and looked startled, apparently noticing for the first time the full extent of the mud on the duvet. "Boy, I did a number on that, didn't I?" Without waiting for an answer, she added, "I'll call the school now. Kenneth's school. I mean—he and Curtis didn't get along, but still, Curtis was his father and I guess he has to know. Please, will you stay here while I do? In case I—sort of can't tell them?"

She looked at her hands, then, with a startled expression, and went in her bathroom to wash them before coming out to use the telephone.

I might as well not have bothered to stay. She didn't tell the person at the school exactly why she was calling; she just said there was a major emergency at home and Kenneth needed to call her back as soon as possible. And then she looked rather annoyed. "I see. All right, do that. Thank you."

She cradled the handset and then said, "He's gone camping."

"What?" I said.

"He's gone camping. Middle of November, and half of his class is out camping on the Appalachian Trail. It's some kind of wilderness survival exercise. They'll have to have a forest ranger sent in to bring him out and get him to a telephone. They said for me not to expect to hear for at least several hours, and it might be a day or two, because it's been snowing and some of the trails are impassable." She shook her head, ran her fingers through her already tousled hair. "If it ain't one thing it's another. That's what my grandmother used to say. And you know, if you change *ain't* to *isn't* it doesn't sound right.

"Okay, go get your paperwork," she added. "And I suppose it's time for me to improve the shining hour otherwise. I'll be about fifteen minutes, is that okay?"

"Sure," I said. As I left, she was getting underwear out of a drawer and heading for her bathroom.

I did not let her apparent calm or her attempts at humor deceive me; I had seen the tears repeatedly welling up in her eyes, seen the determination with which she forced the tears to stop. She was still extremely fragile, and I might still have to re-call the ambulance for her. But certainly a shower was a step forward (and in a momentary flash of memory I saw Jackie Kennedy, standing in her pink suit still spattered with her husband's blood, her eyes dazed with shock and horror, as Lyndon Johnson took the oath of office on an airport tarmac. She must have had other clothes on the plane. Why didn't someone *make* her change clothes? But I'd read somewhere that loving friends had tried to get her to change clothes, and she'd screamed something like, "No! I want them to see what they've done to me!").

I had just stepped into Curtis's room when Patrol Officer Andrew Jackson's voice from downstairs yelled, "Hey, Detective Ralston, did you want a veterinarian?"

"Yes, but tell him to wait just a minute," I yelled back, and told Habib what Jeanne had told me.

"Well, he didn't die anytime before five-thirty, that's for sure," Habib said. "So it doesn't matter how soundly she slept. Okay, go talk to your dog doctor. Sorry I snapped at you a while ago. It's just that Dane"—Dane, I knew, was Dane Patrick, M.D., a new addition to the M.E.'s staff— "is out sick, and I have calls stacked up the wazoo."

"Yeah, he's completely zonked, okay." The veterinarian, a blond woman with short hair and bright blue eyes, let go of Polka's eyelid, which she had pulled up to look at one eye. "And you need to know what with?"

"That's right," I said, ignoring Captain Millner, who was glaring at me.

"Where's his identification? It ought to be on his collar, and he looks like he normally wears one, but—"

"His name is Polka, and he's four years old," I said. "I've got his collar, but I can't let you have it. His owners are—" I stopped and swallowed; my attempts to mentally depersonalize Curtis weren't working so well. "His owner is Jeanne Minot. She's upstairs taking a shower."

The vet was making notes on a paper form. "And the police need this information? Well, that's good enough for me. I don't think dogs have rights to privacy, though the animal-rights crowd would probably pillory me for saying that. As far as the owner's right to privacy, well, I'll let you worry about that." (I wasn't worried. I was pretty sure whatever was in

57

Polka's bloodstream was covered by the consent-to-search form Jeanne was going to sign. Of course, she hadn't yet, so if she changed her mind I might have a problem or two, but I didn't think she was going to change her mind.)

"Now, Polka, you just be a good dog—" The veterinarian found a vein in his left foreleg, tied a rubber tube about halfway up it, tapped the vein below the tube several times with the back of her middle finger, inserted a needle, and filled a vial with blood, then another and another. "That ought to be enough. And he's starting to wake up, so he ought not to need any more medical treatment. If he does, call me again or take him to his regular doctor—he does have one, doesn't he?"

"Yes," I said, "but I don't know who."

"Where should I send the report?"

I gave her my card, and she left. "What," demanded Captain Millner, who had been a silent observer, "was *that* all about?"

"How many times do I have to explain it?"

"One more than you did already. I want it in writing tomorrow. Right now I don't want to know why you need to find out what zonked the dog. What I want to know is, why didn't you just let Habib take the blood and run the tests?"

After a moment I managed to say, "Because I didn't think of it. Anyway, I don't think he'd appreciate the implication."

"What implication?"

"That he's a dog doctor."

Millner tried not to laugh.

Polka started coughing then, and I got him off the couch, but not out of the living room, before he began barfing, which I had long since learned the hard way is how dogs normally end a coughing spell. Fortunately I was carrying him on the bathroom rug, so that it was easy to put Polka *and* the rug out in the backyard.

I had failed to remember that Bob was working in the backyard. He yelled something that was fortunately incoherent except for my name, and I brought Polka, who was now rather woozily walking, back in. I left the rug outside and washed Polka's face and chest thoroughly with soap and warm water, then rinsed with more warm water, before turning loose of him. He immediately started shaking the water off, liberally spraying me, and then he tried to run into a room in the downstairs northeast corner of the house, but was blocked by a closed door.

He whined briefly at the door and then went up the stairs, his nails clicking on the polished hardwood, to whine and scratch outside the closed door of Curtis's bedroom. When the door was not opened, he tried to make an end run into the room through the bathroom, but the door from it to the hall was closed. He returned to the bedroom door. There he planted himself firmly on the floor and whined and whined and whined, only varying with an occasional plaintive yelp.

There was no budging him from there, and I could not dog-march him by the collar because, of course, at this time he had no collar he could wear. So I sat and petted him and finally he curled up and dozed off in front of the door, still whining in his sleep. He'd have to be moved later, when it was time to remove the body, but for now he was all right. As far as being safe from people falling over him, anyway. Dogs can smell a lot more things than people can, though, and I had no doubt that he'd smelled the death of Curtis Minot. His conscious mind—however much conscious mind dogs have; I've heard a lot of discussion over that—might not understand, but his subconscious knew quite well what he was smelling.

Then I went downstairs to check on Sue's coffee, which was ready, and then I went upstairs to check on Sue, who was asleep. I closed the door of the guest room—excuse me, Kenneth's room—that she was in, and went back to the chair I'd been using in Jeanne's room.

Her trash can was now empty and unlined. I went to check, and Bob told me that Irene had collected its entire contents and wanted the duvet also. "She'll give it back if it proves not to be evidentiary," he said.

"Well, be sure Irene knows that Jeanne found the body, and that when I got there she was lying across his bed shaking him, with blood on her hands, trying to wake him. And then she went and lay down on her bed with her jacket partly under her. So I don't know what could be evidentiary. I can account for anything that got on any of the clothes or on the duvet."

"You know Irene," Bob said.

I know Irene. Her persistence is usually a good trait, so the few times it isn't we try to ignore it.

I went back to check on Jeanne, who had lain back down on the bed. I hated to wake her if she'd managed to doze off, but sooner or later I was going to have to.

I would have to decide whether I was here as friend or as cop. Trying to be both at once was confusing me, despite the fact that I had been in similar friend-or-cop situations several times in the past. Unfortunately, just as in the previous situations, I couldn't see any possible way I could separate the two. There's only one of me, and it was busy.

# 3

JEANNE WAS AWAKE; SHE SAT UP WHEN I reentered the room. She was now in clean slacks, shirt, and socks, and she asked me to help her with the duvet, which she'd shoved off on the floor. Obviously it wasn't washable. The two of us together managed to fold it, with the blood and mud on the top so that it wouldn't be able to get on the rest of it, and she set it neatly in a corner of the room. "I'll get it to the cleaners when I have the energy to think about it," she said. "And if it's ruined, it's ruined. I don't suppose it matters much now."

"Actually, Irene wants it," I said. "And she's already taken everything you put in the trash can in here."

"Who's Irene?"

"The crime scene technician. She wants to check and see if there's any useful trace evidence on it."

"I don't know what would be," Jeanne said, "but she's welcome to it. On second thought I don't want to send it to the cleaners. I don't want it anymore. Just tell her to get rid of it when she's through."

She looked back at the duvet. Her face tightened; then, very determinedly, she got an old nylon-quilted bedspread out of the closet and, with my help, laid it over the bed. Then she sat back down, in socks and no shoes, crosslegged on top of it. "I'm going downstairs after a while," she said. "Is that okay?"

"Of course; why wouldn't it be?" I answered, slightly startled.

"I mean, I won't be in anybody's way?"

"If you are, we'll ask you to move," I said. "Believe me, Irene never has any problem with telling people to move, or, for that matter, with telling people off."

"Good, because I'm getting hungry. Is it crummy for me to be hungry?"

"I can't see how it could be," I said. "I think people usually get hungry when there's a death in the family. That's why the tradition of friends bringing in food got started."

"I doubt I have enough friends to bring in much food," Jeanne said. "We never stayed anywhere long enough to have friends. And I don't have a job, and we don't go to church, and we don't belong to any clubs, and—how *would* I meet people? I've been so glad to know you." She grabbed a tissue, wiped her face. "All right. I'm all right now. You said something about paperwork? Things you need me to sign?"

I got the couple of forms I'd put on her dresser and gave them to her. "They should be self-evident," I said, "but if you have any questions about any of them let me know. Officially I'm supposed to explain them all to you, but I'm pretty sure you can read."

She smiled a little, fleetingly. "Yes, I've been reading for a long time. And Curtis did allow me to have a library card." She signed the consent-to-search form and handed it over to me to witness. She paused then, looking very puzzled, and then held up the Miranda form. "Why this?" she asked. "I'm not a suspect, am I?"

"Of course not," I said. "The best that anybody can tell, you were jogging with me when it happened. But unfortunately in just about any kind of murder other than a random violence or murder in the course of robbery, the first person you have to look at is the spouse, and I don't want some judge jumping down my throat next week because I didn't tell you your rights. Which means I have to ask you to sign this and be sure you understand what it means. If you—well, not you, but if, say, somebody didn't want us to search a crime scene we would just get a search warrant. No judge would have any trouble issuing one. But nobody ever is *required* to talk with the police, especially if there is even the slightest possibility of the person incriminating himself or herself. So you couldn't tell us to go away, but you could tell us you didn't want to talk to us, or you didn't want to talk to us without an attorney. And if you couldn't afford—"

"I understand what it means," she interrupted. "And money is not what I'm short of. If I needed an attorney I could pay one." She looked doubtfully at the form, shrugged, signed it, and handed it to me. "Now what?"

"We want to search the whole house, because we don't know where in the house the perp might have gone."

"The perp being the—the murderer?" Tears began to trickle down her face again.

"That's right," I said. "We need to search Curtis's bedroom very thoroughly, along with any other place in the house where he might have kept paperwork."

"He had a great big study downstairs," she said. "It's in the northeast corner; I don't think you've ever been in it."

"No, but I know where you mean," I said. "Polka was trying to get in there, and I didn't know why."

"That's why. This time of day, that's almost always where Curtis would be, and Polka is emphatically his dog, not mine or Kenneth's. Polka makes that very clear. Anyway, most of his—Curtis's—paperwork is there, and his safe and file cabinets and so forth. One of the computers is down there and the other is in his bedroom. He had somebody rig them up in a way that he could access both computers from either room. A network or something like that."

"We'll get to that later," I said. "Do you have the combination of the safe?"

"No," she said, and hesitated. "I might—I think I might know where he kept it. You want me to look?"

"Would it be in his room or study?"

"Yes. I mean it could be in either one, but it's usually in his study. I think it's in his Day Runner, disguised as a telephone number."

"Then let's wait until the rest of the searching has been done."

"The executor of his will has it, of course. The combination, I mean."

Feeling vaguely surprised that Jeanne wasn't the executor, I asked, "Who's that?"

"Ken Rimer. Sue's husband. But I can't get ahold of him today; he's some sort of commercial traveler, I don't know what in because I don't think he's a salesman; but anyhow, he's on the road today. He almost always is Monday morning through Thursday night."

"We'll reach him later, then. Another thing I need to know—" I hesitated. "What *did* Curtis do for a living? I mean—" Oh no, Jeanne had said *I mean* so many times that I was catching it. I decided to rephrase. "I know he was retired, but before he retired? You said something a while ago about your presence cramping his style—"

By now I was pretty sure I could answer that question myself. What I was really after now was the matter of whether or not Jeanne knew her husband's business.

She closed her eyes briefly, then opened them again. "He was always putting together deals," she said. "He never did work like in an office; he never did have a secretary. He wouldn't even let me do his typing and stuff; he did it all himself, and he kept his computer files locked, so you may have a lot of fun trying to get into them. Even I can't get at them."

"Ducky," I said, hoping that Captain Millner, who persisted in believing that I had learned all about computers in the month he gave me to do it in, would not expect me to use an unfamiliar network or access locked files.

"He did have an accountant," Jeanne went on, "but I don't know if even the accountant knew the source of the money."

"So you don't know what kind of deals he was putting together?"

"Oh, some of them," she said. "Like, he'd find a gasoline refinery, usually a small one, that had produced more gasoline than it turned out to really need during some period of time, and he'd put together a deal to sell several tank loads of it to some small independent gasoline stations for a few cents a gallon less than they'd have to pay their usual supplier. Or he'd find a company that had discontinued some line it was producing, and he'd arrange to buy all they had left and then he'd sell them to discount houses, mail order or regular stores, depending on what it was and how much was left. Or he'd find some militia outfit or rifle team that was disbanding, and he'd buy up all its guns and sell them to somebody else. And sometimes—there's this way people can buy scrap metal from the military, only a lot of times perfectly good parts are in there designated as scrap. He'd buy lots of those and go through it pretty thoroughly, and sell what really was scrap to a steel mill or something like that and keep the rest, to put with other good parts he'd get other times, and you'd be surprised at some of the things he and Ellis were able to put together."

"Such as?" Of course the name had caught my attention; Gerry Scamander had mentioned Curtis and Ellis as having a telephone quarrel recently.

"Such as—I mean, I can hardly believe it, but stuff like helicopters and guided missiles, and these really humongous guns."

I would like to have been able to disbelieve that. Having recently seen a television show on that very topic, I couldn't disbelieve it. "What did he do with them?"

"He sold them different places. I don't really know. He didn't talk about that kind of stuff with me; I wouldn't know if Ellis hadn't mentioned it one time when he was here, and right away Curtis told him to shut up."

"Did he have a federal firearms license?" I asked, thinking of Bran, who'd complained about rusty guns—Bran, who might be, but was not necessarily, Irish. No firearm license by itself gives anybody permission to sell firearms out of the country; that takes a lot of special permits which cannot be obtained if the importing country doesn't want the firearms imported. Of course, no number of laws, no amount of enforcement, was going to keep illegal sale of firearms, smuggling of firearms, from happening, any more than the surveillance of border patrols and coast guards of just about every country with a coast or a border—which includes every country—had ever been able to prevent smuggling of everything from garden plants to plutonium.

"What's that?"

Jeanne's question snatched me back into the now; what was she asking about? Oh yes, a federal firearms license. "It's a government license to sell firearms."

"Oh . . . I remember him talking about one once, but I don't remember what he was saying. Mostly he and Ellis, and Ken before he bailed out, used to just talk about the spot market."

"The stock market?" I wasn't sure I'd heard right.

"No, the spot market. I don't know what that means."

Neither did I, but I had a hunch that Harry, who had recently received his MBA, would know.

Jeanne added, "Deb, let's go get a sandwich or something. I mean"—her face clouded up again—"even if it is my fault—and it is—I'm still hungry. And if that's ratty of me then I guess I'm just a ratty person."

"Jeanne, you are not a ratty person," I said, but as I could have predicted, she tuned that out.

# 4

We wound up making tuna salad, with pickles and celery and onions and sliced tomatoes and mayonnaise and those little yellow-green Italian peppers I always like so much, and sitting in chairs in the formal dining room eating sandwiches and potato chips; Jeanne had coffee and I had water. "I just don't want to be upstairs," she had explained apologetically. "So we can't watch TV because the TV is upstairs."

She offered me hot chocolate but I didn't feel the taste would go with the taste of the tuna. We offered everybody else sandwiches but nobody else wanted them except, of course, Polka, who had temporarily given up waiting outside Curtis's door and now daintily accepted everything that either of us offered him. The phone occasionally rang but we ignored it, as Captain Millner had appointed himself telephone monitor and was answering every call.

But there is a limit to what one can ignore. When Captain Millner came into the dining room with a certain degree of relish, I had a hunch I wasn't going to like what he was going to say.

I was right. I didn't. He said, "You've got to be in court at one o'clock. I'll drive you."

"Are you out of your mind?" I demanded. "Look at me! Sweats, no shower, messy hair—"

"I'll drive you home, then," he said. "You can get dressed and take your own car downtown. What are you worrying about? It's just twelve-ten. And it won't take you over twenty minutes to get downtown."

Even Jeanne laughed at that. There are some things that men just do *not* understand.

"Before you go," Jeanne said, "would you mind very much getting that Valium from my room? I—I'm sorry, I know I'll get over it, but I just—I don't want to go upstairs right now. And I think—I think maybe I'd better sleep. I mean—I can't even plan the funeral, not until they tell me when the funeral home can have the body."

I felt sympathetic; it couldn't be easy for her to try to behave normally with her husband's body still upstairs, from whence it would not be moved until the crime scene people were completely through. I went up to her room, noticing in passing that the duvet was also gone now. Collected as evidence, I assumed. Well, if I'd been doing the crime scene, I'd have collected it too. Even if, like Irene, I had already been told it couldn't possibly be evidentiary.

I left Jeanne wrapped in a crocheted afghan, a homey-looking cover in her formally elegant house, lying on one of the couches in the living room.

In the car on the way to my house, Millner said, "He *had* a federal firearms license."

I could hear the stress on the word *had*. "What happened?" I asked.

"Revoked. For dealing in illegal weapons."

"Such as?"

"Full automatic assault rifles, after the ban went into effect. Also weapons with serial numbers filed off. Also sawed-off shotguns. Also silencers and silencer kits. To say nothing of military matériel. He hadn't been indicted yet, but he would have been soon and he knew it. My guess is he was headed straight for the federal pen in Atlanta. And that code Scamander said it sounded like they were talking in? It *was* a code."

"Phone taps?" I asked.

"Phone taps. Legal, on warrants issued by a federal judge. Dub wants us to keep him posted on the investigation, in case something comes up he might need to get in on."

Dub, whose real name was William T. Arnold, was an FBI agent. He and I had frequently worked together on joint city-federal cases, partly because it seemed to amuse our respective superior officers to have what was sometimes called the "Dub and Deb Show."

"Also—shall I go on, or do you get the picture?" Millner asked.

"I get the picture," I said. "And I think the FBI had better take a good long look at everybody with access to the tap and the tapes, because *somebody* knew Jeanne was leaving very early this morning. Look, if you insist on me working this case, I've got to do the search in the victim's room and office, and that means somebody's going to have to sit on the scene until I get back."

"Somebody will," he said. "What about his wife? It's going to take several days to get a full search done; if she stays here then we've got to keep somebody here all night every night until we're through. Do you think you could talk her into going somewhere else? Most women would want to, but she doesn't seem to."

"She doesn't believe in ghosts," I said. "No, I probably can't, but I'll try. But you'd have to keep somebody there all night anyway." Like me, he had no illusions that strips of yellow crime scene tape really kept people out. "Oh, and you're going to have to get somebody to drill the safe—"

"We can't find the combination?" he interrupted.

"Not yet, anyway. Sue's husband is supposed to have it, but he's on the road and can't be contacted. Jeanne says she might know where it is, but we're not there yet, and anyway if it is there it's disguised as a telephone number, so even if we figured out which one it was we won't know which way to turn the dial to what numbers. And I was trying to say, we need somebody else to break into his locked computer files."

"Why can't you do that?"

"Because I'm not a hacker. Trust me on this one."

He shrugged. "I guess I've got to. I just don't see how it can be as complicated as you're making it out to be."

He stopped at my driveway, and Pat, our pit bull, charged out of his doghouse barking wildly until he noticed that the unfamiliar car had brought me home. Then he started wagging his hindquarters, which is what dogs who have almost no tails wag. I scratched him behind the ears and unlocked the front door, which hadn't been locked. By the time I figured out why I had to turn the key the other way, Harry had opened the door, and Ivory, our accidentally acquired cocker spaniel, was leaping between Harry and me and putting his paws all over my sweats. Then he charged past me and went out to play with Pat, except that Pat charged past me on the other side to get inside the house, which brought Ivory back inside also. Our old calico cat, Margaret Scratcher, who was sitting on the coffee table, hissed and slapped Pat, who rebounded, yelping, as he always does, and then did nosies with her, which is the other thing he always does after she scratches him.

Rags, who was on top of the television set and therefore was top cat at the moment—cats seem to have this rule that whichever is sitting on the highest piece of furniture has the most status—yawned widely and went back to sleep.

Sometimes I think we have too many quadrupeds.

"How come you're still home?" I asked Harry after we both got indoors.

"I took the day off, after you called me. I thought you might need me."

"I always need you." I leaned against him for a moment, and then said, "But alas, so does the court system. I've got to be downtown by one. That gives me about two minutes to shower and dress, considering I've got to find a parking place."

"I'll drive you," Harry said. "That'll cut off ten minutes. After I drop you off I'll go over to the library and wait for you there."

That meant I would have to walk about a mile from the courthouse to the library, after the judge decided he was through with me. I had already run five miles today.

So what?

Unfortunately, in the shower I started thinking. Thinking of Jeanne's grief, thinking of the fact that I couldn't even think of anything to say that would comfort her.

Someday Harry would die and leave me a widow, unless I died first.

What could anybody say to comfort me?

And even if I did die first, what would that change?

I was crying when I exited the shower, and Harry said, "What's wrong, Deb?"

"Just thinking about Jeanne," I got out. "What would I do if I lost you? What if we weren't married anymore?"

"Hey, hey," he said, "you're not going to lose me, so what are you crying about? We've been married for twenty-six years, and I told you when we got married that it was for life."

"That's what I'm crying about," I told him.

He didn't know what I meant by that. And that was the rest of what I was crying about.

# IV

THURSDAY, NOVEMBER 11, TO
FRIDAY, NOVEMBER 12

# 1

THE JUDGE HAD THE BIT IN HIS TEETH; we were going to finish this trial today or else. I was through testifying by two-fifteen, but I might be needed for re-direct, re-cross, or rebuttal, so the court decided to keep me. Neither the judge nor any of the attorneys asked me whether it was convenient for me to stay. But then, they never do.

If there is anyplace in the known universe more boring than a witness room, I haven't found it yet. If you're confined to—excuse me, sequestered in (we must speak the lawyers' language)—a witness room, even if there are other people there you can't talk about the case or anything even vaguely related to it, and there's a bailiff present to make sure you don't. If you want something to eat and/or drink, another bailiff will go and get it and bring it back for you, but you can't go get it yourself. There is a rest room at the back of the witness room, so you can't even wander down the hall to the rest room. I have crocheted afghans by the dozen while waiting to testify or retestify, but I hadn't brought any crocheting with me today. I have read scads of books, but I hadn't even thought to bring a book with me today. At one point we—the several other confined witnesses as well as I—had tried playing shuffleboard on the floor with pennies and straws, but we soon gave that up: without a table to play it on, we were not being kind to our backs.

We sat.

And sat.

And sat.

Captain Millner came in about five and told me the body had been moved to the morgue, and the funeral home could have it around noon Friday. He'd told Jeanne, he added, so I didn't have to. Then he said that Harry had called the office: he had to leave the library and go home, so as to pick up Cameron, our five-year-old son, from the day-care center where he goes after kindergarten on the days when Harry and I both have to work. "I'll be around awhile longer," Millner said, "so if you're not too late I'll take you home. If you are too late, get somebody to drop you by the station and take a detective car."

"What's going on at the crime scene?" I asked.

"Nothing much right now. I told you they took the body, and we're through with the main crime scene work. We've got a computer expert"— he still looked disappointed at that; obviously he continued to cherish hopes of being able to turn me into a computer expert—"and a safe expert going to meet you at the scene at eight o'clock tomorrow morning."

Eight o'clock. Goodie. I could hardly wait. That meant Harry would have to take Cameron to kindergarten again tomorrow. Not that he wasn't perfectly capable of doing so, but I like to be the mother every now and then.

As the interminable hours dragged on I began idly watching a late-season fly buzz around the ceiling of the witness room. There was a spider web in one corner, with a spider waiting patiently, and I was wondering which would happen first: the fly would fly into the light fixture and fry itself, the fly would fly into the spider web and turn into fast food for the spider, or the judge would let me go home.

The case finally went to attorney summations at eight-thirty (the fly was still alive). All the witnesses could leave; the unfortunate jurors, I supposed, were stuck for the night. Again.

By now, Harry would have already attended to supper and

put Cameron to bed, Lori—the fiancée of our missionary son, Hal, who had been living with us since her mother's death— would have gotten home from work and would be in her room frantically doing homework, and Harry would be on the computer, on any one of the several networks he still subscribes to despite the fact that at least three of them now offer full internet access. So I didn't feel the urgency I had felt earlier to get right home. I'd eat somewhere on the way, I decided, and then just check in on Jeanne, assuming she was at home, as she probably was.

I called Harry to let him know what was going on, and he said, "Jeanne Minot wants you to call."

"Did she sound urgent?" I asked.

"No, she just wanted to ask you something."

I would call Jeanne. Of course I would. Maybe I'd even drop by her house. But it was a quarter till nine o'clock, and so far that day I'd had a tuna fish sandwich, about six potato chips, and a glass of water. I was going to get some food.

Sometimes my ideas are not as good, or even as well thought through, as one could wish.

# 2

I T WAS NINE-THIRTY WHEN I PARKED THE unmarked police car at the curb in front of Jeanne's house. Jeanne let me in herself; the patrol officer who'd been left to guard the scene was sitting diligently on a dining-room chair knitting in a place where she could see the front door, the back door, the door to Curtis's study, and the staircase; and Polka, who like all Dalmatians actually needs about a seven-mile run every day though he rarely gets it, was rushing about making a pest of himself. He tried to slip past me and run out the front door, but—used to Pat's ploys to get into the house, and somewhat more alert than I had been earlier in the day—I put my knee in the way to block him until I could get the door closed. "Sorry it took me so long to get here," I said, "but I was kind of stuck in court and then I had to grab a bite to eat."

"That's okay," she said. "Really, you could have just called. I know you're worn out, and I wouldn't even have tried to call you, except—it's just a little puzzling."

"What is?"

"Well, about five o'clock Ken—not Kenneth, my son, but Sue's husband, that Ken—called and asked where Sue was. I was still asleep on the couch—Officer Raye had to wake me, and of course I was surprised because I thought Ken was still on the road. He said her—Sue's—car was there but she wasn't. And—I couldn't figure out where she would have gone, especially without her car. So I just wondered, did she tell you anything?"

"No, last time I saw her she was asleep in—I thought it was your guest room, but I guess it must be your son's room."

"I didn't even think of looking there," Jeanne said. "I think—I think I thought she'd gone home. Surely she did. She would have, wouldn't she?" Her face was slowly paling; realization was beginning to hit her. "But Deb—that was—" She glanced at her watch. "It must have been close to ten hours ago."

"Closer to twelve," I said grimly.

We headed for the stairs at the same time, with the uniformed officer—one Tamera Raye, Andrew Jackson having gone off duty—directly behind us.

We couldn't get in. The door was locked from the inside, and as usual I was the one who wound up picking the lock with a bobby pin. I was surprised Jeanne didn't know how—most mothers do, as a result of the proclivity young children have for locking themselves in bathrooms—but maybe she'd had a nanny when Kenneth was that age. And Tamera Raye didn't look old enough to have children; she also didn't look old enough to be a police officer. I suppose it's a sign of my age that more and more presumably responsible adults look like children to me.

I held my musings to that, trying not even to imagine what we would find inside the room, though I was pretty sure I knew. What, that is. Maybe not how. Probably not when, exactly. And especially not why.

It was really a very simple lock, which clicked open under my hand after no more than a couple of minutes.

# 3

I STILL DON'T KNOW EXACTLY HOW IT WAS done, and I don't have a clue as to why. I don't suppose I ever will know, because the only person who knows won't tell.

The bottle of Valium, which I had last seen in Curtis's bathroom, was on a table beside the bed, empty. So was the bottle of Flexeril, a prescription muscle relaxer. So was a bottle of digoxin, a heart medication which, according to its label, had been refilled a week ago, by the AARP pharmacy, with one hundred tablets. So was an empty glass which, from its dregs, appeared to have held water and a few other things, things that had gotten powdery from being water-soaked.

The digoxin, according to its label, belonged to Jeanne. "I didn't even know it had come," she said, sounding dazed. "I'm still on the old bottle."

"That's yours?" I said, rather stupidly in view of the fact that Jeanne's name was on the label. "You've got a heart problem? Then should you be jogging?"

"Oh, sure," she said. "It's nothing serious, just a little arrhythmia, barely enough to need treatment—but how did she get it? When did it even get here?"

It didn't take me much glancing around to find a white Tyvek package addressed to Jeanne Minot, thrown at but not into a trash can in the corner of the room. "What time does your mail usually come?" I asked.

"About ten o'clock. Sometimes as late as noon, but not often, and never later."

I was *here* at ten o'clock, and also at noon. So were about seven other police officers. I couldn't remember any mail arriving.

But obviously the mail had come, and somebody had taken the package from the mail, and the two open bottles from Curtis's bathroom, and brought them into this room and emptied all those capsules and dissolved all those pills in the water, which to my mind wouldn't leave very much room in the glass for water, and had somehow forced/cajoled/tricked Sue into drinking that devil's brew. Presumably the person had then departed, locking the door behind himself or herself.

I didn't know how long it would take for all that junk to work. Presumably, since so far as I knew she hadn't eaten, she'd had it on an empty stomach, and that much Valium by itself would have put her unconscious very quickly. That much digoxin—well, it was safe to assume she'd died because her heart stopped beating. The difference between a therapeutic dose of digoxin and a lethal dose is pretty small, and she'd had—apparently—one hundred times the therapeutic dose. "Where did this glass come from?" I asked Jeanne, who was almost but not quite breathing down my neck and sobbing quietly again. A cheap glass printed with Dalmatians—more than one, but fewer than a hundred and one—didn't seem to fit Jeanne's elegance.

"It was in the bathroom. It's one Kenneth likes."

So Sue hadn't had to leave the room to get a drink of water. That locked door was bothering me, because it wasn't locked when I had looked in on her early in the morning, and I was asking myself whether she could have absentmindedly, maybe accidentally, or for that matter deliberately, locked it after going out of the room and then returning.

All that was assuming that Sue had committed suicide. But why? So far as I could tell, there was no possibility whatever that she *could* have killed Curtis, even assuming that she would have had a reason to kill her twin brother, and although after the body was discovered she had seemed as stunned and grief-stricken as anybody would have been in her situation, she had not appeared, at least to me, to have dropped into the kind of despondency that could lead to suicide. And the EMTs hadn't thought she was shocky enough to need to go to the hospital.

The glass was in Kenneth's bathroom, in the northwest corner of this room. She wouldn't have had to leave the room to get it if she'd wanted it.

But she would have had to leave the room to cross the hall, to get Curtis's Valium and Flexeril, and—*how* had she managed to get the package from the mail? Unless it came a day or so earlier and maybe Gerry Scamander took the delivery, but if so wouldn't he have given it to Jeanne or put it with the rest of the mail? But if that had happened Jeanne would know, and she'd said she didn't know, and besides that, with Jeanne's near-fetish for tidiness—without even seeming to think about it, she'd put a clean bedspread on her bed while her husband's body was lying across the hall—she'd never, no matter how carelessly, have put that Tyvek package where I found it.

Sue wasn't a slob, but she wasn't as neat as Jeanne. She could have tossed the package at the trash can and not noticed that she missed it, especially if the drugs were already taking effect and she was feeling fuzz-headed.

Sue could have locked the door behind herself before drinking if this was suicide, but—

Wait a minute. Wait a minute.

This couldn't be suicide, not that I really thought it was anyway. Once again, it was murder disguised as suicide, and not very well disguised.

If Sue were going to kill herself this way, she'd have swallowed the pills and capsules with the water, several at a time. None of them were large. She could probably swallow five or more at once, and considering she'd be swallowing about two hundred tablets and capsules, she'd have probably done it in the bathroom, where she could get more water as needed.

If she'd taken the Valium first, on an empty stomach, she'd have been nearly asleep by the time she swallowed the last of the pills. Would she have bothered to take the glass and put it beside the bed?

And even if she had, that wouldn't have left dregs of unswallowed, incompletely dissolved tablet crumbs and the smaller debris dumped from capsules at the bottom of the glass. It's generally safe to assume that drugs that are routinely enclosed in capsules taste extraordinarily nasty. No, she'd have swallowed the capsules, not dumped them into the glass.

I took a couple of steps into the bathroom attached to this room, and looked in the toilet. Yes, there were undissolved capsule containers in it, clearly taken apart and emptied before being dropped into the toilet. It appeared that somebody had tried to flush, but the gelatin of the capsules was by then just wet enough to be very sticky, and the water of course was too cool to dissolve the capsules quickly.

How long had it taken to do that?

Many years ago, when I was in ident, I'd been detailed with Bob Castle to destroy some drugs. It was recommended to us—as it probably would not be now—that we destroy them by washing the powders and fluids down a sink in the janitor's closet, breaking open each vial and dumping its contents down the sink, and running enough hot water to dissolve all the capsules.

The drugs had a wholesale value, to the hospital from which they had been stolen, of about three hundred dollars. After they had left the hospital and spent at least two nights lying in a pillowcase on top of a grave in a little-used old cemetery, the hospital wouldn't take them back.

Their street value would have been between two and ten thousand dollars, depending on how much the cocaine in two of the bottles was cut.

It took us four hours to finish that job, and by the time we were through, both of us were sort of crazy from the fumes and powders floating around the room.

How long had it taken this killer to prepare the solution that Sue presumably consumed?

How had *anybody* had the nerve to stand in here at the sink with police in the house, with Sue in the adjoining room, long enough to dissolve the tablets, empty the capsules, and put the glass where she'd find it and drink from it?

The whole thing stank to me, and I couldn't help remembering a suicide I'd worked many years ago. A young woman had—I don't know what to call it, controlled, intimidated, coerced—her husband into doing everything her way by threatening suicide every time they quarreled. When that got too old for him to pay any attention, she started "attempting" suicide. She would go to a motel, call somebody and tell the person to tell her husband the car was in front of such-and-such motel and she'd be dead, and then dramatically swallow pills. I can't imagine why anybody would do that more than once—having one's stomach pumped can't be much fun—but she got away with it about seven times.

Then one day she called the wrong friend and left only a partial message—that her husband should be notified that the car would be at the motel.

This was a new friend, somebody who hadn't known her more than a couple of weeks, somebody who didn't know her behavior pattern.

Before she swallowed her pills she got her hair done, she made herself up beautifully and skillfully, and she wore a pretty pale-blue negligee and arranged herself artfully on the bed.

Unfortunately, the new friend talked with her husband and the two of them agreed not to get involved with the neighbors' fights. If the neighbor woman had a fight with her husband and went off somewhere and left their car at a motel, they could sort it all out themselves when the woman got through being mad.

The woman wasn't found until four days later. By then, that nice hairdo and pretty makeup and frilly negligee didn't do a thing for her.

Then there was the addict who'd decided to take the

easy—he thought—way out. But he'd choked on his last hand-ful, and he didn't die the way he had planned to die: the sticky gelatin capsules were still lodged in the back of his throat, blocking his windpipe, when we found him. An overdose isn't as easy a way out as a lot of people seem to think.

Sue didn't kill herself. Somebody killed her.

Somebody killed her in a house that at that time contained her sister-in-law and anywhere from one to eight—depending on when it happened—police officers, possibly including me.

I hate locked-room mysteries.

The kind in books, usually by John Dickson Carr in one of his multiple personæ, are fun, because they usually involve about fourteen different people doing about thirty unlikely things each so that the situation winds up as it does.

In real life, they usually happen by accident. Something goes a little bit wrong, and something that was quite possible looks temporarily impossible. In the one locked-room mystery I'd had in the past, the answer when I reached it turned out to be very simple. It would with this one also. I was sure of that. But it might take me a while to get there.

Of course, the most obvious suspect in both killings was Jeanne. But not only could I think of no conceivable reason why she would have done any of it, to the best of my knowl-edge she'd been downstairs constantly since before I left. And anyway, there was that empty package on the floor beside the trash can. In my experience, people are themselves no matter what the crisis; in major crises they're even more themselves than they are normally. I'm pretty messy at times, mainly be-cause I have about twice as much to do as any one human being *can* do in the time available, and in a crisis I tend to be-come even messier. Jeanne would become even tidier; even if I hadn't known that before I would have realized it as I watched her tidying her bedroom earlier that day. She—if she had poi-soned Sue—would have automatically thrown the package in, not beside, the trash can, and probably would not even have noticed what she was doing. She wouldn't have *thought* of putting the package anywhere but in the trash can, even to throw suspicion off herself, because untidiness is not present in her mental universe.

I hadn't touched anything in the room, including Sue. There had been no reason to. Now I began backing away slowly, just enough that Jeanne, behind me, was forced to back away also. "Tamera," I said to the uniformed officer, "call dispatch. Tell them to get me a complete homicide crew out here. And have them notify Captain Millner."

As soon as she was off the phone, I called Harry.

# 4

$I$T WAS HERE-WE-GO-GATHERING-NUTS-IN-MAY time again. It was déjà vu all over again. It was Arnold King, M.D., from the medical examiner's office pronouncing the victim dead—ballpark it at five hours ago, around five P.M., he'd said, and if she'd taken even a tenth of the stuff it appeared that she'd taken, she'd have died fast—and M.E.'s investigator Ramona Hunt taking photographs; and Sarah Collins from ident doing fingerprint checks; and Captain Millner downstairs attempting to explain to Kenneth Rimer, Sue's husband, what had happened; Rimer for some reason then getting the bit in his teeth about opening Curtis's safe right that minute, only Millner wouldn't allow him to do it; and Andrew Jackson and Gerry Scamander downstairs looking sleepy; and Philip Greene, Curtis's night nurse, asking whether he was going to get paid for coming out only to find his charge dead and the house full of police, going home and going to bed early for a change, and coming back out again on a moment's notice. "It might be a tacky question," he admitted, "seeing as how Curtis is dead, but look, I've got to make a living."

"I'll pay you!" Jeanne screamed. "I'll pay you, now will you please *shut up?*" She wiped her eyes, blew her nose, threw her tissue at a trash can, missed, got up and walked over to the trash can, picked up the tissue and dropped it in, and returned to the couch. "Please just shut up," she said, more quietly. "Tell the police what you know, and then go away. I'll pay you to the end of the month. I'll pay you to the end of *next* month, if you'll just shut up now."

Then she clasped both her hands over the top of her head and said to the room at large, "I'm sorry, but look, I don't think I can handle much more today."

That, I could well believe.

"Why don't you go out and get the dog?" she said then to Greene. Polka had managed to get past Captain Millner and was running around outside having a grand time. As he'd now been gone over an hour, there was some possibility he might be willing to come in.

"Is that okay?" Greene asked.

Nobody answered at first; then I said, "Okay, but if you can't find him come right back in."

So far it had been established that:

At no time between the time I left to go to court and the time I returned to see what Jeanne had called me about did Jeanne go upstairs. This was not just her assertion; it was also the assertion of Patrol Officer Andrew Jackson and Patrol Officer Tamera Raye. A trace metal detection test, done at Captain Millner's suggestion (to "clarify matters," he had put it delicately), proved that Jeanne had not had a gun in her hand at any time in the last twenty-four hours, unless she wore gloves.

There were no fingerprints on any of the pill bottles or on the drinking glass; Sarah was going to have to take the Tyvek package to the ident lab to work on it, because it was a difficult material.

Sue's fingers had strong and distinct ridges and should have left good clear fingerprints. Jeanne's ridges were smaller, but they also were firm. She too would have left good clear fingerprints.

At no time between the time I left to go to court and the time I returned did Sue go downstairs. Again, word of police officers, not just word of Jeanne.

Nobody would admit to having brought the mail in that

day, and in fact there was mail in the rural box out by the street.

When the last of the police other than Tamera, who was staying all night, had left, Jeanne had checked all the windows upstairs and down and then re-armed the security system.

Obviously nobody could have murdered Sue Rimer.

Obviously somebody had done so, all the same.

# 5

BACK IN THE DAYS WHEN I DRANK COFFEE, I'd have been up to about my sixteenth cup by now. As it had been well over two years since I had drunk any coffee as well as twenty-one hours since I'd been in bed, I was all but walking in my sleep.

Both nurses, as well as Patrol Officer Andrew Jackson, had gone home. The medical examiner's crew was gone with the body, and Captain Millner was gone, and Kenneth Rimer was gone, protesting to the last that he had a right to open the safe. Captain Millner had repeated, as many times as Rimer had protested, that certainly he had the right to open the safe, but not yet. Jeanne, who appeared to have decided to put the upstairs off-limits to herself for sleeping purposes for a while, was once more lying on the couch wrapped in an afghan, watched over by Tamera Raye, who was knitting again. Polka, having run about the neighborhood for two hours, was now asleep outside the door to Curtis's room. I was just about to go home, as soon as Sarah stopped poking around doing whatever it is that ident people do now—I'd been in the ident unit for a while, but that was a long time ago and some procedures had changed.

It was past two A.M. by then, and I was distinctly startled when I realized that Jeanne, Tamera, Sarah, and I had suddenly been joined by a weedy-looking boy who seemed to be about ten or eleven years old. He was short and thin, he had thick glasses, and he had that kind of crease on his nose that people get who have perpetual allergies. "What's going on here?" he asked in a rather nasal voice.

Jeanne came straight up off the couch. "What are you doing here?" she screamed. "You're supposed to be in Maryland!"

It did not take all of my detecting skills to realize this child must be Kenneth Minot.

"I was in the TV room," he answered indirectly. "I went there first, and then later I couldn't go to my room because Aunt Sue was asleep in it. And with all those cars parked in front, I figured you were having a party or something, so I stayed out of the way. But I'm hungry."

By now my jaw had dropped about a foot. In the TV room? The TV room was in the southeast corner of the top floor of the house, and I personally had checked it and found nobody.

"You're supposed to be—the school said you were—" Jeanne was gabbling.

"Oh yeah, the hike." He shrugged. "I didn't want to go on it. You know I hate that school. All that let's-all-go-make-like-tough-guys stuff."

"Maryland—"

"It was easy. I told Coach Hopkins I had an earache and couldn't go on the hike. I don't think he believed me, but he just told me to go to the infirmary. He doesn't like me anyway; he thinks I'm a sissy, but I'm not. So he didn't care that I wasn't going. Then I didn't go to the infirmary. So the infirmary thought I was with Coach Hopkins and Coach Hopkins thought I was in the infirmary. I figured they'd have found out already, because once I got home and found out what had happened I figured you'd have tried to call me, but maybe you didn't. They'll find out Sunday anyway when Coach Hopkins gets back, but I don't care. I hate that school."

"But—*Maryland*—"

It was evident that Jeanne was stuck on the fact that the school was in Maryland, which is quite a long way from Fort Worth, Texas. It was also evident that Kenneth was more resourceful than either of his parents had given him credit for being.

"I hitchhiked." It was a throwaway line, almost sounding rehearsed, and he headed for the kitchen.

"But you—what time did you get here?"

I was glad she asked. I wanted to know, but I couldn't ask without giving a Miranda warning.

"About six-twenty," he said from the kitchen. "This morning, I mean. This guy I hitched with, he let me out on the highway a little after five, and I walked the rest of the way. I saw you leaving." I heard the unmistakable sound of bread being put in a toaster as he went on talking. "I was wondering how I was going to get in, because I didn't have my house key, but then I found the gate open and so I just went in a window—"

"But the security alarm—" Jeanne interrupted.

"It didn't go off. I moved a bale of hay over and climbed in through the breakfast room. I got in easy enough—all I had to do was just shove the window open and crawl in. Then I went in my bathroom and took a shower and then—I was sore, I fell about eight times last week rope-climbing at school and they kept making me climb the stupid rope again, so I went in Dad's bathroom and got about three Valiums and took them. I heard Dad cough while I was in there, so I left fast in case he decided to go to the bathroom."

"Curtis has been coughing a lot lately," Jeanne told me.

"Well, he wasn't coughing a lot then," Kenneth said. "He just coughed once. And then I heard somebody walking around so I figured Gerry had come early because of you leaving early, and I didn't want Gerry to find me. And so I went in the TV room and hid under the couch—"

A cough? And then somebody moving around? Kenneth had probably heard the murderer, I thought, and that gave us a time. But what had muffled the shot that much? Too bad Kenneth didn't look into his father's room, though of course if he had he might have been killed too, so it was probably best that he didn't.

"*Under* the couch?" Jeanne interrupted, her thought processes not at all in line with mine. "I don't think there's six inches of clearance—"

"About eight, actually," he said. "And I can get pretty small when I try."

"But why did you—"

"Because I figured you'd want to clean all the bathrooms when you got home like you do every day—which I think is really stupid, by the way, considering most of them don't get used—and I was pretty tired and I didn't want you to find me until I'd gotten some rest. So I went to sleep, and later I decided I'd sneak into my room. You know, like you can get kind of tired of sleeping under the couch. But like I said, when I woke up and went in my room Aunt Sue was there, so I went back in the TV room." He was still out of sight in the kitchen.

"Kenneth!" Jeanne called. "I tried to phone you at school. I did try. Your dad—your dad is dead."

"Oh yeah, I heard that on TV a while ago while I was waiting for your guests to go away." I heard him open the refrigerator. "I couldn't figure out why you'd be having a party right after dad died—I was glad he died, but a party this soon would be kind of pushing it."

Even I felt somewhat stunned by what I was hearing. Jeanne said weakly, "It wasn't a party. Kenneth, your father was murdered, don't you understand that?"

"Doesn't bother me," he said calmly, popping open a Coke can. "If it wasn't a party, what was it? All those cars." He raised the can to his mouth, and I could see every swallow going down.

"The police," Jeanne said. "The police, Kenneth. All those cars were the police. And don't drink like that; you'll choke yourself to death."

"Never have yet. And if he died this morning, how come there were still police here tonight? Did they just now take him away? I looked out the window a while ago and saw somebody go out and it looked like they had a body bag, but he must have been dead an awful long time, I mean, for me to hear it on television, and you wouldn't think he'd be left here that long. Especially if you were having a party." An increasing smell of burnt toast was accompanying his voice around the partition.

"I told you I wasn't having a party! He died this morning, and they took the body away a little after noon. The bag you saw a while ago was your Aunt Sue."

"Oh yeah?" He peered around the partition between the kitchen and living room, a paring knife and a slab of cheese in his hand. "You mean she got knocked off too? Why would anybody want to do that?" I heard the toaster's pop-up sound, and Kenneth vanished again and then, about two seconds later, yelled, "What did you do to this *toaster?*"

By now the burnt-toast smell was floating through the house. Jeanne rushed to open a window, and, of course, the security alarm, which I hadn't realized she'd reset after letting everybody out who was leaving, went off. That caused a little more commotion, after which Kenneth said, "You had the toaster set wrong." He put more bread in it.

He had not, I observed, asked why anybody would want to kill his father.

This was quite a wake-up call.

And the puzzle had a whole new piece, and now the shape of it didn't seem to be at all what I had thought it was.

# V

FRIDAY, NOVEMBER 12

# 1

---

SOMETIMES INSUFFICIENT SLEEP CAN BE even worse than no sleep at all. Insufficient sleep was what I had, considering I actually got to bed about three-thirty in the morning.

But all the same I was up at seven, somnolently making pancakes, which surprised everybody in view of the fact that normally we have cereal for breakfast except on weekends.

As usual, I opened the canister of white flour first, looked at it, said something along the lines of "ick" when I noticed that it was infested with weevils (usually, in our household, called "weasels" as a result of linguistic confusion that occurred when our now-married older daughter, Vicky, was about seven), dumped it into the garbage can and set the canister aside to wash, and wondered why I buy white flour anyway, except that I know I buy it because Lori, for some reason totally incomprehensible to me, likes to cook with it. I got out the whole wheat flour, poured a couple of cups of it into the blender, and added the other things necessary to create pancakes, while the electric griddle heated.

Once we were all seated around the table I asked Harry what a spot market was, and he paused with a forkful of pancakes and syrup halfway to his mouth. "It's—uh—uh, it's hard to explain, sort of. How about an example?"

I agreed to an example.

"Okay, suppose you're shopping at Albertson's. You know what you're going to find there, because Albertson's has standard orders of everything from its suppliers. You know there's always going to be about the same amount of everything you found there last week at the same time. But take that discount grocery store you like to go to. You never know from week to week what you're going to find. The reason is that some supplier sent a fax, or maybe picked up the phone, to the owner of that store and said something like, 'Well, I've got fourteen cases of cream-style corn almost out of date at so much per case, you want them?' And the owner says, 'Yeah, sure,' and the supplier ships them. Most businesses operate on regular orders at regular times, but in some fields of industry, spot market is about all there is and, in some situations, about all there *can* be."

"Like in illegal arms shipments, or drug smuggling?"

"I don't know that much about drug smuggling. Arms, yeah. Except that in this case the would-be buyer might call the potential supplier and say something like, 'Hey, I want three cases of AK-47s, can you get them?' And the supplier says, 'Let me find out.' Or maybe the supplier has three cases of AK-47s, and he might call a contact at the IRA and a contact in Iran and a contact in Peru and say, 'Hey, I've got three cases of AK-47s, what'll you give me for them?' And then the highest bidder gets them."

I thought about that for a while, and then the conversation turned more directly technical, as it sometimes does, with me asking Harry—who is sort of a soldier-of-fortune wannabe and reads all the survivalist and militia catalogs and magazines—the details of silencers, about which I know less than I probably should. "What kind of a silencer?" he asked.

"I don't know what kind of a silencer. I don't even know that there *was* one. I just think there might have been."

"What kind of a gun, then?"

"A 9 mm semiautomatic. Pending autopsy reports, that is. That's what was there, but I can't swear yet that that was what was used."

"Well, the way a silencer is made is—"

"I don't need to know that," I interrupted. "At least not now. I just need to know how quiet one can get."

"On a 9 mm pistol? With a good one, you couldn't hear it from here to our bedroom door."

I turned, mentally estimating a length I'd never bothered to measure. "Twenty feet?"

"Twenty feet."

"What would it sound like if you could hear it?"

"Sort of like a harsh cough."

"Then that would work." *Kenneth said he heard a cough. One cough, and then somebody walking around.*

"What would?"

"I've got to find out how Curtis was killed with people there."

"It's easy, if the killer doesn't mind getting caught."

That, I knew. A Secret Service agent had once told me that just about anybody could kill just about anybody else, including the president of the United States, if he didn't mind getting caught or killed after accomplishing the deed. "This person would mind."

I'm not sure Lori had heard a word we were saying, as she was reading the newspaper while shoveling Cheerios—she'd decided not to have any pancakes—in at a great rate. But Cameron asked, "Who got killed? When?"

"Just somebody I know," I said.

"Somebody I know?"

"Not somebody you know. Just somebody I know," I assured him.

We have to be careful what we say to, or around, Cameron. This past Easter, as I had attempted to explain to him what Easter is really all about, he asked in lively horror, "Somebody *killed* Jesus?"

When I said yes, he burst into tears. "But he was my best fwiend!"

It took a little while to get the rest of it across to him. Then he wanted Jesus to come visit us.

I don't remember whether I asked that kind of question when I was five. If I did, I don't know what anybody told me.

Lori left in her car; Cameron departed in Harry's crew-cab truck, carefully placed and buckled down in the backseat to be safe from air-bag deployment.

I didn't have to go to the office in downtown Fort Worth; all I had to do was go directly to Jeanne's house, eight blocks away, where a safe expert and a computer expert were to meet me. That gave me an extra half-hour at home by myself.

I took the time to put the dishes in the dishwasher and start it, put a load of laundry in the washing machine and start it, and spiff up the living room slightly. Maybe at some point I would get the chance to return the few blocks home—maybe for lunch—and get the laundry into the dryer and start another load.

I did all this very absentmindedly, as the main part of my mind was devoted to figuring out not *who* the murderer was but *how* the murderer had managed to accomplish this deed.

I only hoped that this case wouldn't wind up as maddening, as unsolvable, as certain other cases I'd worked on.

# 2

You do not—if you have good sense—question a twelve-year-old boy at past two in the morning, with or without his parents' consent and/or a Miranda warning. Accordingly, I had not done so.

You also do not question said twelve-year-old boy at eight in the morning, when he is sleeping the sleep of the (presumably) just.

I had a lot of questions I wanted answers to, but they'd have to wait at least until Kenneth awoke and ate breakfast.

He was asleep in his mother's room; according to Jeanne he'd have been perfectly happy to use his own, since Sue's body had already been removed, but Jeanne was not willing to let him. Curtis's room remained completely off-limits, with yellow evidence tape across both the door to the hall and the door to the bathroom. The only reason there wasn't any tape across the door to Kenneth's room was that Sarah had decided there wasn't anything else to do there.

But several things were certain: Unless Curtis had been killed during the two or three minutes between the time that Jeanne left the house and the time that Kenneth entered it—in which case the killer would have still been there when Kenneth entered—he(?) couldn't have gone out the front door and locked it behind himself, at least not unless he had a key, because it had a good deadlock. This in turn meant that the shot had been fired while Jeanne or Kenneth, one or the other, was there. That meant a silencer, or it meant Jeanne or Kenneth was the murderer.

I had tentatively concluded that neither was the murderer, but that Kenneth heard the murderer. That still left the question about how the killer got in, and then back out, without triggering the alarm. I knew the alarm was set when we arrived after jogging, because I watched Jeanne unset it. But we had the word of Kenneth, assuming that he was telling the truth, that the alarm was *not* on when he went in through a kitchen window.

Furthermore it now appeared that it was Kenneth, not the killer (assuming that Kenneth was not the killer, and I wasn't completely sure I could safely assume that), who had opened the breakfast room window.

That left me with the distinctly unsettling picture of a killer who could open the deadbolt of the front door, set the alarm on standby until after he committed the murder (during which time Kenneth must have entered the house), and reset the alarm just before leaving the house and locking the deadbolt. I knew from earlier visits with Jeanne that there was a forty-five-second lag: when the alarm was set, it allowed everybody forty-five seconds to get out and lock the door. After that, it would go off if someone locked the door *or* unlocked it unless the correct code—which changed frequently—was punched in within forty-five seconds before or after the lock was used.

And the next problem was, Sue definitely had been killed while both Kenneth and Jeanne were there, along with at least one police officer and possibly a good many police officers of whom I felt fortunate that I apparently was not one. That meant Kenneth or Jeanne, one or the other, almost had to be the murderer—but why?

But if it was one of them, how was it done?

And if it wasn't one of them, how was it done? Any scenario I could imagine had several steps missing. My imagination is one of my strongest points—sometimes Captain Millner thought it too strong—but for the life of me I could *not* figure this one out.

Any investigator in his or her right mind, as I presumably am, would say that the evidence pointed to Jeanne and/or

Kenneth, either acting alone or both acting together. But unless Jeanne was a far better actress than I thought she was, she was genuinely astonished by the entire course of events. And Kenneth? I couldn't decide yet whether he was really that unconcerned or whether he was acting a role. I had tentatively decided he'd been taking lessons from television on how to be a jerk; since I don't know much about television jerks, having very little time to watch television as well as no interest in jerks, I wasn't sure which one.

There are, I am told, plenty of jerks to imitate.

A time or two I had worked cases in which a friend was a victim, but I had never before worked a case in which a friend was the most logical suspect. (In the one case in which a friend was the perp, I didn't suspect her until the last moment—the very last moment, because she was dead five minutes later, from suicide, leaving me to explain to her daughter as many of the reasons as I could figure out.) This situation—long-range suspicion of a friend—was making me distinctly uncomfortable.

I didn't have enough to take to the D.A., which fortunately meant that no one from the D.A.'s office would be breathing down my neck asking why I hadn't asked for an arrest warrant. I also didn't have enough to be sure I didn't have to continue looking at either Jeanne or Kenneth or both of them together.

If I had to make a bet as to whodunnit, I'd put my money on Kenneth. Tentatively. I could be wrong. All of my conclusions could be wrong, because about two-thirds of them were based on the assumption that all the witnesses were telling the truth. That is very rarely the case, though I wouldn't go as far as Agatha Christie's Hercule Poirot and insist that *all* witnesses lie.

It was fairly safe to assume that Kenneth would have the key to the deadbolt, but how would he know the security code, which had been changed several times since he left for school in the end of August?

Would Kenneth, or Jeanne—

Have a silencer?

Know how to make a silencer?

Oh, that was a ridiculous question. Anybody who can use the internet can find out how to make a silencer, and I had no doubt at all that Kenneth knew how to use the internet.

But why?

And if he was guilty, why the air of insouciance? Surely if he'd murdered his father he would have sense enough to act concerned if not totally grief-stricken.

There had to be another answer, and I had to find it. It would be fairly safe to assume that *anybody* who might have the key to the deadbolt quite possibly might also know the security code.

I was beginning to feel as if I were trying to swim through Jell-O. Nothing in this case made sense.

Because we now had reason to believe that Curtis had been involved in illegal weapons sales, Captain Millner had arrived at the house about the same time I did, with a search warrant specifically allowing us to open the safe and the locked computer files, as well as to search the house and all outbuildings and vehicles.

After excusing Tamera, who'd been there all night, I sat down with Jeanne. Lieutenant Gary Hollister, who was technically my boss except that he spent most of his time with the cases Captain Millner didn't get called to, was wandering around in the backyard with Millner, surveying the scene and probably getting practice for the promotion everybody in the department was just about sure he would get when Millner retired.

Even if they hadn't been here, I could guard the scene quite well enough until the department got somebody else out there.

"You didn't need that," Jeanne said when I handed over her copy of the search warrant. "I already signed that consent form." She moved over slightly on the couch, pushing one of the silk cushions behind her back.

"There could be a problem with that," I told her. "Legally you can give us the right to search the parts of the house that are under your control, and that normally would not permit us to search Curtis's bedroom and study. Since he's dead, it normally *would* permit such a search, but the problem is that we now have reason to believe that we're likely to turn up evidence of crimes that he has committed. And although as parent you're technically in control of Kenneth's room, a case could be made that Kenneth really is. And we have to prepare for every possible eventuality."

Her eyes intent on my face, she slowly began to turn pale, as she had done the day before. "What kind of crimes do you suspect Curtis of?"

"Those deals that he put together. We now have reason to believe that at least some of them were illegal."

"But—"

"And," I added, "there's an outside chance that some of his records might implicate you, or there might be things here that would implicate Kenneth, perhaps in one or both of the murders. That's a chance we—as police officers—can't take. Thus, a warrant."

"But Deb, you know me, do you think I'd go around breaking the law?"

"No," I said, "but legally I have to proceed on the assumption that you might." That gave me the cue I needed. "It would really be helpful if you and Kenneth would agree to take polygraph tests. That way I could totally rule you out—"

"But they're not permissible in court, are they?"

"No, but they weigh pretty heavily in pre-court proceedings. Particularly since I do know you, my judgment in this matter is to some extent suspect. Jeanne, look at it from the law enforcement point of view. You or Kenneth was—were—I hate grammar—one of you, almost certainly Kenneth, was definitely present in the house when your husband was shot. And both of you were definitely present in the house when Sue was poisoned. I haven't a ghost of a reason why you'd want to harm either one; I have a pretty good idea of why Kenneth might want to kill Curtis but not Sue. But you're an intelligent woman; you've got to see that it looks bad. If I could tell the D.A. something like, 'Okay, I know what it looks like, but we ran them on a polygraph and they came back clean,' then I'm much more likely to get the kind of latitude I need to continue to work on the case."

"Well, it's okay with me," she said, "but I don't know about Kenneth."

"You might want to consult your attorney—"

"I don't need to consult an attorney. I didn't *do* anything. And Kenneth—that's bravado. He does that sort of thing. Like last night, he was all set to go sleep in the bed Sue died in, because he thought it would make him look like a tough guy— not the kind of tough guy Curtis and that school wanted to make him, but a different kind of tough guy—and he's really not tough at all. He's sensitive, and if he had really slept in there he'd have been up screaming with nightmares three or four times during the night. About three years ago Curtis and Ken—Sue's husband—took him deer hunting, and he had nightmares about it for six months. And Curtis got that deer dressed out and put it in our freezer, and he wanted venison once a week at least until it was all gone, and he made Kenneth eat that venison every time I cooked it. He'd eat it and vomit, eat it and vomit, and Curtis kept making him eat it. It was after that that Curtis decided to send him to military school, hoping that would toughen him up."

"Why do you think he ran away from school?"

"He hates that school. He always did. I've been trying to find a better one for him, but the problem is that several of Curtis's hot-shot buddies—Daniel Ellis, for one—have their sons there, so he was convinced it was the right place for Kenneth too. Or else it wasn't the right place for Kenneth but it would be as soon as Kenneth changed and turned into somebody he isn't and never will be."

"Do you really think he hitched all the way home?"

She shrugged her shoulders. "I don't know. I suppose he could."

"One time my son and his girlfriend ran away for a few days," I said, "and they didn't have any trouble getting rides. But they looked older than they were, partly because Hal is so big. Kenneth, if anything, looks younger than he is."

"I know. And I see the problem. But all the same he *did* get home."

"Would he have told you if he had heard a shot? Or suspected hearing one?" I had a hunch this question was now immaterial, but my hunches are not always right. "He mentioned hearing a cough, and a gun with a silencer can sound a lot like a cough."

"I don't know," she said wearily. "I do know Curtis had been coughing the last few days. Do you want to wake Kenneth up and ask if he's sure it was a cough he heard?"

"Let's let him sleep. You mentioned a Daniel Ellis. What do you know about him?"

"Just that he and Curtis put together a lot of deals. And his son Grover is in Kenneth's class. I've met him, but I didn't like him much. Daniel, I mean, not Grover. And most of the deals were long-distance. All of them, really, since Curtis's accident."

"Would Daniel Ellis have had a motive to kill Curtis?"

She shrugged again and then began absently rubbing her left shoulder with her right hand.

Left shoulder. What was that making me think of? "Jeanne," I said, "did you take your heart medicine today?"

"No, but that's okay. If I miss it a day or two it doesn't really matter much. I told you it's just a little arrhythmia."

"Tell me where it is and I'll go get it."

"Deb, I told you—"

"I know what you told me. And I know you're under extremely heavy stress. Where is it?"

"Oh, all right, it's in the drawer beside my bed."

I went upstairs, got the entire bottle, and brought it back down, giving the bottle to her with a glass of water from the kitchen. She swallowed the tablet and set the glass down beside the bottle. "You asked if Ellis would have a motive to kill Curtis. I don't know. I really don't. I know Ellis was mad at him about something, but nobody would tell me what, and Curtis never cared if somebody was mad at him. He'd just laugh. But Ellis—I don't know. I doubt he'd have had a chance, anyway. After all, he is in Maryland."

"So was Kenneth, day before yesterday. It didn't take him long to get here, hitching. It wouldn't take Ellis even that long if he flew. Do you think Kenneth had a reason to kill his father?"

"I don't think he would have," she said evasively. "You saw what he was like last night. He—Kenneth—didn't like his father. He had no reason to like him. But—I didn't see any rage there; I haven't since right after the thing about the venison. It was more like he'd just turned Curtis off, like in his mind Curtis just didn't exist anymore. I mean—Curtis would tell him to do something, he'd do it, but he'd do it like his mind was in Siberia. He quit—reacting—to Curtis's bullying."

"On the surface," I said.

"On the surface," she agreed.

"What was going on inside, below the surface?" I asked.

She fidgeted a minute, running her hand across pale gray-green silk slub over and over as if the cushion were a pet, and then asked, "What would happen if I confessed?"

"Did you do it?"

"You didn't answer my question."

"You didn't answer mine. Look, Jeanne," I said, "police get false confessions to a lot of crimes. They come for a lot of reasons. Sometimes the person just wants his five minutes in the spotlight; sometimes he's so mentally off he thinks he really did it or caused it; sometimes he's protecting somebody else. In this case the immediate question would be, who were you protecting? And the answer would be Kenneth. And he'd wind up under more suspicion rather than less."

"I can't convince you I did it?"

"I don't know, but I don't think so."

"But you couldn't prove I didn't do it," she said.

"I probably could, actually. On Curtis, anyway. Maybe not on Sue."

She looked puzzled. "How would you do that?"

I started to answer, but the doorbell interrupted me. Jeanne turned off the security system she'd turned back on after letting me in—I didn't know why, in view of the fact that two people had already been killed in this house despite the security system—and I opened the door. A grizzled, middle-aged man in gray chino work clothes said, "I'm Roy Elton. I understand there's a Gary Hollister here who wants a safe man?"

"Yes. I'm Detective Deb Ralston, and I'll need to be there when the safe is opened."

He came on in, carrying what looked like a small piece of luggage, and asked, "Whereabouts is this safe?"

"Down this hall," Jeanne said. "Deb, do you want me there too?" She was automatically rekeying the alarm system as she spoke, so, of course, it went off again when Captain Millner and Gary Hollister tried to open the back door to come in.

That little commotion ended fairly quickly; Jeanne—after some urging from Captain Millner—agreed to leave the system on standby; and we all went down the hall toward Curtis's study.

Elton got there first. He opened the door to the room and then turned to me. "Ma'am, this safe is already open."

The rest of us pushed around him.

The safe was open. Not just unlocked, not just cracked open, but all the way open. A rather large amount of American currency was in it, all used bills, all neatly banded; later, on counting it, we would find four hundred and sixty thousand dollars there. And nothing else. No notebooks, no papers of any kind.

And the computer the computer expert was supposed to break into?

It wasn't there.

Oh, the monitor was there, and the printer, and a lot of cables. But not the main part of the computer. And no floppies, on or in desks, tables, safe, or anywhere else so far as we could see.

# 3

THE SAFE EXPERT, OF COURSE, WAS GONE. The computer expert still hadn't arrived, and it was well past nine o'clock.

Oh well. What good would the expert be if we didn't have the computer?

When we started trying to decide who was the last person who'd seen the safe locked and the computer in place, we finally concluded that nobody had looked in that room since 0945 on Thursday. That provided somebody plenty of time to come in and take the computer away—provided he could find his way past four thousand square feet of pyracantha, a sophisticated security system, and a phalanx of police officers.

Why, I wondered, did he bodily take it away, instead of simply wiping the disk, which would have been far easier?

But there are ways of getting information off supposedly wiped disks. I wasn't knowledgeable enough to use them, but I knew they existed. Obviously he or she—whoever—didn't want to take the chance, which also told me that he was not enough of an expert to be able to make a drive totally unreadable, but he knew enough about computers to know how much he didn't know.

But—

How long had Curtis had two computers?

Did the killer know he had two computers?

The killer ought to have been able to spot the computer in Curtis's bedroom, except that I had never seen one there, and I'd been there several times before entering it when Curtis was dead. So where was it? Was the killer likely to know or guess?

Had Curtis backed up each computer's hard drive on the other computer's hard drive?

I turned and ran up the stairs, ducked under the yellow plastic tape, dashed into Curtis's room—and did not see a computer.

But I also did not see anything a computer would have been likely to sit on. This interested me.

I opened the top of the rolltop desk and found no computer. I opened one storage wall door and found no computer, another storage wall ditto, and a third storage wall door—and there was the computer, its green ready lights glowing as if its owner had left it just for a second rather than forever.

The killer had finally goofed—I hoped.

# 4

THEY'RE SOPHISTICATED LOCKS, MA'AM," the computer expert said. "It's going to take me a while to get into them. I hope you understand that I have to go slow, because if I don't I could inadvertently wipe the disk completely."

"Take as long as it takes," I answered. Gary and Captain Millner had both left, and Andrew Jackson was back on guard; this time he was watching from a patrol car at the curb across the street, which gave him a view of every possible entrance that did not involve going through pyracantha. Bob Castle was wandering around taking pictures of an open safe and of an empty computer table; then he began fingerprinting windowsills. After a while he went outside, and then he came back in and said, "Deb, I want you to look at something."

We went outside together, where it immediately developed that I was too short to look at his something.

He went and got the ladder from the crime lab truck, where he had returned it after he finished doing the fingerprints and photography in this area, and brought it over and I climbed it.

I was looking at the outside of the dining room window.

Just at the level of my hand was a loop of electrical cord.

"I don't know for sure how he got in the first time," Bob said, "but this is how he got in the second time."

"I don't see what you mean."

"The loop of wire. The way the security system works, if a circuit is cut by a door or window being opened, the alarm goes off. But he used this loop of wire to create a short circuit—not what you think of as a short circuit, when something quits working, but a real short circuit. The circuit that was supposed to go around this window now goes under it. He probably got up on a wooden ladder and wore thick rubber gloves and used heavily rubber-handled tools, cut a piece out of the glass to get at the wire, routed around the circuit and hooked in the new wire before detaching the old, and went in that window as easy as cutting pie. I'll show you. Go tell that lady to re-arm the security system."

That took about two minutes. Then, when I returned to announce the work completed, Bob confidently opened the window.

Very easily.

The security system didn't even squeak.

In addition to the circle of glass cut out high in the window, a small circle had been cut out right by the window lock, and the lock itself disengaged by hand; it didn't need a key. The two glass disks had apparently been taken away, as we never did find them.

The window was open, and Bob climbed inside it. "Oh yes, oh yes," he said then. "This is it."

"*What* is it?" I demanded from the ground.

"Come on up and you'll see."

Moments later I was scrambling in the window, to find myself standing directly beside the elevator that went up to the second floor. "See?" Bob said. I suppose I must have looked baffled, because he said impatiently, "The elevator. He could get up to Sue's room using the elevator, and nobody downstairs would even hear it."

"Those cuts in the glass weren't there yesterday," I said.

"I know," Bob answered. "I checked it yesterday. But I don't remember whether the loop of wire was there. I don't think it was."

"I don't either. I think I'd have noticed. But I don't know."

Bob motioned me toward the elevator, and not wanting to

play "After you, Alphonse; after you, Gaston" for several minutes, I stepped on over to the door.

Bob pushed the button (yes, of course it had already been checked for fingerprints). Completely soundlessly the elevator door slid open. We both stepped inside. Completely soundlessly the elevator rose; completely soundlessly the door slid open again, and we were in the upstairs television room.

My locked room mystery was no longer a locked room mystery. Whether the killer had gone after Sue on one trip and then returned later to get the computer, or whether he'd done it all in a single trip, it was obvious how he did it. No matter how many cops were in the living room, after the main investigation team left there was nobody who would have seen, from the inside, anybody going in this window or up the elevator, and the chances that anybody would see him walking across the hall into the room where Sue slept were small. There was minimal risk of his being seen at the dining room window, because of the cedar tree; if any of the neighbors saw a man carrying a ladder to the window they'd almost certainly have assumed the man was one of the investigators.

There might be a little more risk in his stepping across the downstairs hall and back with the computer, but if he watched his time carefully—oh, it was doable. It was very doable.

Locking the door to the room Sue was in would have been easy enough; all he had to do was push the button and then close the door.

If any of us had heard the water running upstairs we wouldn't have noticed. We'd just have assumed it was Sue.

If Sue had a habit of waking up thirsty and grabbing the glass beside the bed for a drink of water—if somebody knew about her habit—oh, yes, it was doable.

Except that Kenneth, according to his own story, was asleep under the couch when all of this must have been going on.

Did Kenneth sleep through a murder?

Or did Kenneth commit the murder?

# VI

---

FRIDAY, NOVEMBER 12, TO
SATURDAY, NOVEMBER 13

# 1

After getting Jeanne and Kenneth to sign releases, and persuading Jeanne to at least call her lawyer even if she didn't want him to come to the house or go to the police station, I had spent about half an hour on the phone with Cubbins, the polygraph operator, explaining the situation and what he could and could not expect (or hope) to get from them, and he had set aside time that afternoon for Jeanne and Kenneth. During that half-hour our computer expert, one Stephen Ramey, had continued to assure me occasionally that the locks were pretty sophisticated and he didn't know how long it would take. Jeanne discarded her antipathy to the upstairs part of the house long enough to come and watch for a while, until Ramey asked her to leave. Then she shrugged and departed.

Kenneth was in the television room, watching junk videos and eating the Chee-tos he'd been escorted by a uniformed officer to buy at the nearby convenience store. If he had any sorrow at all for the deaths of his father and aunt, he hadn't let me see it. More and more my suspicion was directed toward him, because he was beginning to look to me like a possible sociopath—and the definition of a sociopath includes a lack of ability to realize that anybody else is real. If he knew anybody else was real I'd seen no evidence of it. I wasn't even sure whether he knew he was real.

By now the crime scene people had departed after their third trip to this house in about twenty-eight hours, and in the presence of Danny Shea, now a corporal and presumably somewhat more on the ball than last time I met him (though he still wouldn't have been my choice), I was searching Curtis's bedroom. (Ramey of course was there, but he was busy with the computer.)

Although Curtis had made extensive use of computers, I did not believe that he'd trusted everything to a computer or even to two computers. Disk crashes are rare, but it's not unheard of for both computers in one house to crash at the same time—that happened to one of my brothers, who called me, slightly hysterical, one Saturday night to inform me that he had to deliver a paper on Monday, both computers in his house had crashed, and his backups were locked in his wife's downtown office to which he didn't have a key, and his wife was out of town. I sympathized, which was about all I could do about the situation.

Surely Curtis had backup floppies, at the very least. The intruder might have taken the floppies away, or the floppies might be stored somewhere an intruder presumably wouldn't think to look, or the floppies might (as Harry makes sure ours are) be stored in a safe deposit box at a bank.

But I didn't think so.

If he was indeed a gunrunner—and by now I had little doubt about that—then he had to be prepared to leave fast, without computers, if he learned somebody was closing in on him. Obviously his paralysis made this much more difficult, but still not impossible, particularly with a devoted wife to help him.

That, and a lot of money.

The money in the safe, which by now had been counted—had it once been an even five hundred thousand dollars? Did the forty thousand now missing from that figure represent the refund given to the man named Bran?

But that was reaching. I had no real reason to suppose that it had ever been an even five hundred thousand dollars, no real reason except symmetry.

Jeanne demanded symmetry. Not having it would drive

her buggy. But how did Curtis feel about it? Eventually I'd need to find out.

Meanwhile I kept on looking, pausing briefly to talk on the telephone with a technician at the medical examiner's office, who told me the bullet lodged inside Curtis's skull had not been fired from the 9 mm semiautomatic found on the floor beside his bed. It had been fired from a .22 short semiautomatic.

Ducky. We were now looking for a different gun from the one we suspected—and a .22 with a silencer would choke down even quieter than a 9 mm with a silencer.

Eventually I'd have to get enough people out here to search this entire house, but right now I didn't want to look for the pistol. I was looking for documentary evidence, though if I found the .22 I wouldn't, of course, complain.

I closed the drawer I had just finished and opened the next one down, telling Shea to note what I was doing and when I was doing it.

Shea was not searching. Shea had exactly one role today—witness. When I needed measurements he would hold the other end of the measuring tape. When I needed a second set of initials on collected evidence, he would provide the second set of initials. He would keep the evidence collection log but I would verify it before we left the building, probably before we left the room. And in court, if this case ever went to court, he would say that I supervised everything he did, he witnessed everything I did, and yes, sir, he had discussed his testimony with somebody else, namely the district attorney and me, and we both had instructed him to tell the exact truth. (Naturally, knowing Danny Shea, I was also keeping my own log.)

There are very few things that bother me more than sloppy crime scene work—of the type the entire world had seen in relation to the trial of O. J. Simpson—and sloppy testimony, which includes falling headlong into every trap that defense attorneys set. Most of the traps are pretty common, and there are common, and correct, answers to every one of them; I had virtually writhed with frustration as I watched that silly young evidence technician in the Simpson trial deny having discussed her testimony with anyone, thereby branding herself a liar under oath, in view of the fact that anybody with good sense and probably quite a few people without good sense knew perfectly well that she had discussed it at least with her supervisor and probably with someone from the D.A.'s office.

Jeanne had told me that she knew nothing at all about Curtis's business, nothing at all about where or how he stored information. Did that mean he had put everything away himself? If so, then I had only to look in places a wheelchair-bound man could put things. Except that Jeanne had said he'd go across the floor on his belly like a snake if he had to. So he could reach everything that wasn't up too high. He couldn't stand up; he couldn't stand on a footstool or ladder.

But he could have had somebody else stash something for him, something the contents of which that somebody was ignorant. One of his nurses? If I didn't find anything today then I'd have to talk with both of them again. Actually, I'd probably have to talk with both of them again anyway, but if I could find his non-computerized records I probably would be able to cut down on the required time.

His sister? She was dead; she wasn't going to tell us anything.

Ken Rimer, his brother-in-law and former partner? Maybe, but if so Ken wasn't going to tell us anything. It was quite likely that anything that would incriminate Curtis would also incriminate him.

His other associate, Daniel Ellis? Maybe, but if Ellis was in Maryland that didn't much matter. I'd have to check on that, of course.

His son, Kenneth Minot? Maybe, but from what Jeanne had told me Curtis and Kenneth didn't get along very well. Actually, they didn't get along at all. Would Kenneth go on keeping a secret after the man who had forced him into secrecy was dead?

I didn't know. So far Kenneth hadn't stuck his head out of his bedroom except just long enough to go out and get the

Chee-tos and then to go to the television room, and it was now ten-thirty. Somebody—preferably Jeanne—was going to have to light a fire under him pretty soon, if he was to keep his date with a polygraph.

Jeanne? I'd think she would have told me if something like that had happened, but I couldn't be sure. She wasn't exactly a close friend; we'd spent maybe sixteen to twenty hours together all told, and that wasn't enough for me to feel I could predict her actions.

Meanwhile I was still turning over books and papers, while Shea sat on the bed watching me.

That bed. If I had ever had any questions as to whether Jeanne was a compulsive housekeeper they would have been settled this morning. After everybody including me agreed that the police were through with the bed—getting through with it involved removing all the bedding down to the bare mattress, in case further analysis of any kind was needed— Jeanne, despite having previously declared herself unwilling to come upstairs for any reason, had quite calmly asked my permission, gotten out a clean set of sheets, clean blankets, a clean bedspread, and new pillows, and then remade the bed. Then, for good measure, she went and remade the bed in Kenneth's room.

I do not consider myself a superstitious woman. But anybody who thought I could comfortably lie down and go to sleep on a bed on which a man had recently been shot to death, or a woman had recently died of poison, was out of his or her mind. Who, I wondered, did she expect to sleep there? Surely not Kenneth, who was subject to nightmares?

I'd finished the bedside tables. I still had an entire wall of storage units to go through—no ordinary clothes closets in this household, except for Kenneth's room. The south wall of Jeanne's room consisted entirely of several folding doors covering one large walk-in storage unit; so did the north wall of Curtis's room, so that two storage walls insulated their rooms from each other.

That made me wonder about something. "Shea," I said, "go in the room next door and shut the door. Stand there three minutes by your watch, and then come back."

"Whatcha doing?" Ramey inquired.

"You'll see," I said. I had discovered this trick in an Agatha Christie book, and I'd used it several times before to see whether people in a particular location could hear, from another particular location, sounds they claimed either to have heard or not to have heard.

After Shea left, I closed Curtis's bedroom door, to lessen the likelihood of sound escaping through the door that wouldn't escape through the storage wall. Then I opened two of the doors to the storage area, to allow for ventilation and make sure that air pressure didn't keep me from making as much noise as I wanted to make. I slammed one of the doors shut, as hard as I could. Then I opened a dresser drawer—I say a dresser drawer; actually the drawer was in part of the storage wall—and slammed it shut as hard as I could.

Then I checked over Shea's notes, finding them satisfactory, and then I just stood there until Shea sauntered back in a moment later. "Did you hear that?" I asked.

"Hear what?"

"Did you hear anything happening in this room?"

"No, should I have?"

"That was the question," I told him. "You've answered it. Now go to that room that's kitty-corner across the hall from this one, and shut the door. Come back in three minutes."

He exited, I went through the whole megillah again, and he returned.

The next time I sent him to the television room. "I woke the kid," he said apologetically on his return. "I didn't mean to, but he was probably about to wake up anyway, what with all the noise on that video. I can't figure out how he went to sleep with it going. It's an Arnold Schwarzenegger movie. *True Lies.* That one's pretty noisy, so he must have been pretty tired. But anyway I figure he was about to wake up."

Probably that was true. After all, Kenneth had been in Maryland for several months, and that's one time zone later than it is here. His body would be telling him it was nearly lunchtime and he'd slept, or videated, through breakfast, unless you choose to consider Chee-tos breakfast. I don't.

"What did you hear?" I asked again.

"Nothing," he said. "What was I supposed to hear?"

"That was the question, and you answered it."

"That's just what you said last time."

"So? It's still true. I had a question about what could be heard from here to there, and you answered it for me. That was all I needed. Now let's try the bathroom. Let's find out what you can hear from it."

"Which bathroom? The one right here?"

This time he was back in somewhat less than three minutes. "You dropped something," he said. "Or maybe slammed a door or something like that."

"And you didn't hear the same thing from any of the other three rooms?"

"No. Why?"

"Just take my word for it that it matters. You've answered the question and I thank you."

At least he'd answered the question to my satisfaction. Certainly neither Jeanne nor Kenneth could have heard anything from their rooms if a silencer was used; probably they could have heard nothing even if a silencer was not used. But Kenneth could have heard it from the bathroom where he claimed to be.

That did not make it impossible that one or the other or both of them were lying, though the condition of the dining room window made it clear somebody had taken pains to get in from the outside.

Actually, that was the question that was most crazy-making to me. If our murderer had not come in the breakfast room window, which apparently he had not in view of the fact that Kenneth admitted to having moved the bale of hay and opened the window, then presumably our murderer had come through the front door with the key and the combination. If he could do that, then why would he have come through the dining room window the second time? Just to evade the police? But it would have taken a lot of time, effort, and risk, as well as a ladder, to bypass the security system and cut the glass.

Was the computer even taken by the same person who committed the murders?

Were both murders done by the same person? I was assuming they had to have been—it would be pushing coincidence well past the breaking point for me to assume that after one person killed Curtis another person broke into the same house to kill Sue, who didn't even live there.

Was the murderer the same person who had stolen the computer?

Was the dining room entry made before or after Sue's murder?

Was it made the first time to kill Curtis, and none of us had noticed it?

That was nonsense; nobody, not even Danny Shea, is careless enough to fail to notice pieces cut out of a window glass.

A lot of things weren't clicking, and if I was ever to clear this case I'd have to figure out what and why before I could get to who.

I went on diligently turning things over one at a time; Shea went on diligently watching me. Then he said, "Is it okay if I go downstairs and get a drink of water?"

"Yes, Danny," I said, my voice sounding weary even to me. "Go downstairs and get a drink of water. Get Ramey and me one too. The glasses are in the cupboard above and to the left of the sink."

I should have known. Danny Shea will never, ever, ever learn common sense.

He came racing back without glasses of water but with a large plastic bag full of a dry, leafy green material wired closed with the little red papercoated wire thingy from a bread wrapper. "Look what I found!" he said.

I looked. I also smelled; I didn't need to open the package to know what it was, but I did anyway, for Shea. "Smell it," I said.

He smelled. He looked puzzled.

"Shea, it is *mint*," I said. "Mint does not smell like marijuana. Marijuana does not smell like mint. Okay?"

"Put it back?" he asked.

"Put it back. Next time you think you've found marijuana, or any other contraband for that matter, don't touch the bag. Go and get the officer who is in charge of conducting the search. Let that officer decide what to do with, to, for, or about it. Now, put it back, and then return here, bringing with you the water you went for. Okay?"

After he headed down the stairs, Ramey asked, "He a congenital nitwit?"

"Oh, yes," I said. "He's perfectly capable as long as he's closely supervised. But leave him on his own, especially if he gets excited, and he forgets he ever had a brain, much less what to do with it."

"Doesn't sound like somebody who ought to be in law enforcement."

"You got that right, though I have no doubt at all that he'd have been just as bad in any other job. It's just that in some other jobs horse sense isn't quite that critical. He's not quite bad enough to fire, not yet anyway. And I don't get stuck with him very often."

Shea returned with the glasses of water. I resumed searching.

I was pretty sure, though not totally sure, that whatever I was looking for would not be among Curtis's clothing, because almost certainly somebody else put his clothing away. But just in case, I turned over the contents of very tidy—Jeanne's hand there, perhaps—drawers, finding nothing there but socks and underwear.

I checked inner and outer pockets, hems and seam linings, of all the clothes on hangers.

I skipped the next section of storage wall, because Ramey was working there, and went on to the one after that.

Never mind the rest of it. It was four o'clock and I was technically off duty by the time I hit paydirt, downstairs in Curtis's study in a hidden—not well hidden, of course—drawer inside one of his desk drawers. It had started out to be one of those small green combination daybook and mileage diaries, but it had so many other pieces of paper stuck in that it bulged twice as large as it should. There was a frayed red rubber band around it.

I took the rubber band off and started reading.

Before I had read three pages I knew I had to call the feds. But which feds? There was clear evidence here of gunrunning; that would be the Bureau of Alcohol, Tobacco, and Firearms, part of the Treasury Department. There was clear evidence of illegal imports. That would be the Customs Service, also part of the Treasury Department. There was clear evidence of interstate shipment of stolen gasoline; that would be the Federal Bureau of Investigation, part of the Department of Justice.

I know more people at the FBI than I do at the ATF or at Customs. Apparently it was once again time for the Dub and Deb Show, since I would be working with Special Agent (a title that always amuses me, as the FBI has no ordinary, unspecial agents) William T. "Dub" Arnold. And it was Dub who'd asked to be kept posted.

I called.

Dub was gone, Special Agent Donald Chang informed me. He wouldn't be back till tomorrow morning. Was this urgent—if so Don would get somebody, most likely himself, out right now or patch this call in to Dub at home—or could it wait till tomorrow, since Dub and I were used to each other's investigative methods and Don really was kind of busy?

I decided it could wait until tomorrow. I was increasingly bleary-eyed and well aware that it was late Friday afternoon and I had had only three-and-a-half hours of sleep since I got out of bed at six o'clock Thursday morning.

I finished my search, such as it was—this little notebook was the only thing I had found—and told Shea he could leave but *absolutely instantly without fail* he must go and make his report *immediately*. He assured me that he would, and departed.

I went upstairs to check on Ramey, who apparently neither ate lunch nor got tired. Last time I looked in on him he was humming. This time he was quietly swearing. Apparently the locks were very sophisticated.

He must have heard me come in, because he turned his head and said, "This is a pain in the you-know-what."

"Obviously."

"I'm not going to be able to finish it tonight," he said, "and I don't want to move it, because as minuscule as the chances are, it's not impossible for me to knock the hard drive skitty-wampus moving it. What time can I come back tomorrow?"

"Let me check," I said. We hadn't scheduled a guard tonight, because we'd figured we'd be through here, and we also figured that if Jeanne and/or Kenneth was the target either or both would have already been hit.

I called Captain Millner, who said, "I'm not surprised you're not through. Well, I'm sorry, but all the stakeout people are busy and as much as has been going on out there I don't want to put a uniform there."

"I could—" I began.

"No you couldn't," he interrupted. "I know how tired you are. I slept most of last night. I'll come on over myself."

"But—"

I was going to protest that having a captain guard a crime scene was not a reasonable allocation of manpower or something like that, but he interrupted again:

"I'm curious. I want to know what's going on. Who's there now besides you?"

"Just Ramey. Jeanne and Kenneth went to be polygraphed."

"Oh yeah," he said. "After I get there to relieve you, I want you to come in here. Cubbins says he has something to show you."

I was not pleased. I did not say that I was not pleased. I just asked, "Isn't Cubbins off now?"

"Supposed to be, but he's waiting for you."

# 2

CUBBINS HAD CHANGED HIS DECOR. LAST time I was in his office, he'd had a large Dr. Seuss poster on the wall. It was now gone, replaced by several cap racks, each holding an assortment of "gimme" caps—over a hundred, I estimated without counting, but far from five hundred.

"Not enough room," he said, without asking my thoughts.

I looked at him, and he said, "Everybody always asks why so few. So I tell them before they get around to asking."

"Cubbins," I said, "I would never consider however many caps those are to be few."

"Anyway I had to bring them up here. There wasn't room in the den for any more. I've got a lot of 'em at home."

I suppose if I had a name straight out of Dr. Seuss I'd make jokes about it myself to forestall jokes from other people, so I couldn't exactly fault Cubbins for doing it. But I wanted to go home. "What did you want to show me?"

"This." He unrolled a long strip of paper. "Now, look at these."

I hadn't the faintest idea what those represented, and I told him so.

"Okay, look at these," he said, unrolling another long strip of paper.

I looked. I could see that there were fewer, and smaller, jigs and jags and peaks and valleys than on the first, but that was all I could tell.

"This was Mrs. Minot," he said, pointing to the first one.

"She reacted to everything. Even the test questions, the ones that are supposed to gauge the response comparing lies to the truth. I ask her if she's in Paris, she says no, and all the scales go crazy. I ask her if she's in Fort Worth, she says no, and all the scales go crazy. Totally inconclusive. If I went by what this polygraph said I'd think she'd seen and heard and maybe even committed every crime that happened since the dawn of time and felt guilty about all of it.

"Now, this is the boy. Totally nonreactive. His subconscious can't tell the difference between truth and falsehood. Ask him if he's in Paris, he says no, and everything buzzes right along just as it should. Ask him if he's in Fort Worth, he says no, and everything buzzes right along just as if he were telling the truth. Equally inconclusive."

"Could the boy's responses be caused by Valium?"

"Could, but he said he hadn't taken anything."

"He took 15 milligrams of Valium about eight o'clock yesterday morning."

"Then that's not going to do anything to a polygraph today. Could he have taken any today?"

"Not that I know of. I'm pretty sure not, because the only Valium I know of in the house was used yesterday. What about Jeanne's? Is there any way she could fake that?"

"There are ways to fool a polygraph," he said. "But they're harder than most people think, and most people don't know them anyway. Her? I'd say anybody who reacts like that is overdue for a trip to the funny farm."

"I know her," I said.

"You told me that this morning. You know of any reason she'd be so jumpy?"

"Not except for the fact that two people have been murdered in her house the last two days, one of them her husband and the other her sister-in-law," I said in a rather nasty tone, and then reminded myself I shouldn't take my frustration out on Cubbins. I went on, "I know that she's very orderly. Maybe even too orderly." I told him about her replacing the bedding.

"Think she might be OCD?" Cubbins asked.

"Might be what?" I asked.

"Obsessive-compulsive disorder. That means—"

"I know what that means," I interrupted. "I don't know. She could. I know she likes things to be orderly, but I don't know her well enough to know whether she's obsessive about anything." But I remembered Kenneth commenting this morning about Jeanne's having a habit of cleaning every bathroom in the house every day. "If she is, would that have anything to do with the polygraph results?"

"Might, because if she has strong compulsions she can't carry out she'll be in a constant fight or flight situation. I don't know that it would, just that it might."

"But—let me get this straight," I said. "You're saying it's impossible to tell from this whether either of them is lying?"

"That's what I'm telling you. Her reactions could be consciously faked, but I don't think they are, because in conscious faking there's nearly always a pause, and her reactions are right on the money, less than a second after I spoke every time. His reactions could be the result of medication, but you're saying he didn't have any." He paused for a moment. "You could be right," he added, "because there was one question he did react to."

"Which was?"

"One I just threw in for the heck of it. You'd mentioned the name to me. You didn't tell me to ask about it, but I thought it might turn out useful to you, and so I asked both of them about it. She was off the chart, but she was off the chart on everything else too. But the boy didn't react to anything at all but this."

"What was the question?" I hoped I didn't sound as impatient as I felt.

"I asked him if he knew Daniel Ellis. He said yes. But— look at these spikes."

I looked, and this time I could see what Cubbins meant. But why this reaction?

*Of course he knows Daniel Ellis,* I thought. Whether or not Ellis and Curtis were legally partners, they worked together on a lot of deals. Kenneth went to school with Daniel Ellis's son. So why did the mention of Ellis's name shock him out of his otherwise complete composure?

"I don't know what it means," Cubbins said. "You're going to have to find out. But other than that—nothing. Nothing at all. So I can't tell you yes or no on either of them. I can't even make a guess. Sorry."

I was sorry too. I really would have liked to clear one or the other of them, if not both, not just because Jeanne was my friend but also because it would make my job a lot easier if I could have some idea at least of who not to continue to look at.

Cubbins was heading out the door by the time I got to my own office, to find a memo from Millie telling me the chief wanted an explanation of why I called a veterinarian. So I took care of that, typing it on an old manual typewriter because the computer was down, and because I was so tired I'd forgotten we had tape recorders; and then I dictated a preliminary investigative report onto Millie's tape recorder, the existence of which I had finally remembered; and then I went *home.*

# 3

Ten to six is eight hours. I'd feel a little better if I slept another couple of hours to make up for the sleep I didn't get yesterday, but breakfast awaited me, or the family awaited breakfast, or some such matter. Anyhow, since all the health people now say that cereal with fruit and skim milk is the best thing to have for breakfast, I no longer feel guilty setting out the box of Cheerios, whatever fruit we happen to have around the house, and the bottle of milk.

Actually I could have slept longer, I reminded myself. Even the toughest investigators have to rest once in a while. Cops have days off just like other people do, and I was high enough in assignment and time in grade that I usually got at least one weekend day off, Saturday or Sunday. At the moment things had cycled around to the point that, for a couple of months, I actually had Saturday and Sunday both off.

But cops, like other people, often wind up working on their official days off. Today, Saturday, I'd work, I told myself. After all, I did need to know what was happening. Maybe I could clear it by the end of the day—that was wishful thinking if there ever was any. Sunday I'd take off. Sunday I'd rest.

I couldn't always do that, of course. Sometimes I really do have to work, because crooks work on the weekend. But although we have been told that it is appropriate to get an ox out of a ditch on the Sabbath, I do not consider it appropriate to go and push your ox into the ditch every Saturday so you can get it back out on the Sabbath.

I was in the process of dressing when the telephone rang. Usually a call in the morning is for me, so I grabbed the phone.

"Deb!" Jeanne's voice, clearly recognizable, was even closer to hysteria than it had been over Curtis's murder. "Deb, you've got to come right over, right now, Deb, he's dead!"

"Who?" I asked, trying to juggle simultaneously the telephone and the shoelace I was tying. "Kenneth?"

"No, not Kenneth! That detective! The one that stayed here last night, you know who I mean, I think he's a captain—you said—"

"I'll be right there." I dropped the phone and screamed for Harry.

# 4

I'D CRY LATER.

I'd worked with Captain Millner for close to twenty years, and like everybody else who'd ever known him, I loved him.

Somebody had tried real hard on this one. Somebody had turned into a cop killer and didn't want us to know it. But I did know it, and whoever did it, no police officer in Texas, probably no police officer in the country, would ever stop looking for this one. But the perp, whoever he was, was smart. Getting him wouldn't be easy.

Millner was an old man. Even now, with lifespans expanding constantly in most of the developed countries, sixty-eight is generally considered old. He should have retired a long time ago, but he was just so good at his work. He didn't want to retire, and nobody who worked with him wanted him to.

There was no obvious cause of death; he hadn't been shot, stabbed, or bashed in the head. Somebody wanted us to think this was a heart attack. And it might have been, but if it was, it was induced. I was sure of that not only because of his health—the most healthy-looking people can have unexpected weaknesses, especially in the cardiovascular system—but also because of what I could see in this room.

As I waited, with Harry beside me comfortingly, I was already mentally reconstructing what must have happened.

Captain Millner had figured, as I had figured, that anybody who wanted to kill Kenneth or Jeanne had already had the chance to do it. So if anybody came in, the person would be coming after the second computer. But the only way a person who didn't know about the existence of the second computer at the time he took the first—the only way such a person could possibly have then learned about the second would have been to have been nearby Friday, close enough to see a service truck with the name of a computer repair service on it parked in front of the house all day. By now, if he was computer literate, he'd have already fussed over Curtis's other computer long enough to find those same sophisticated locks that Stephen Ramey had found. He'd have known Ramey didn't take the computer with him when he left, which meant he had to be watching the house from somewhere nearby.

The person who came after this computer would be the same person who had come after the first computer.

That was how I read it yesterday; that was how Millner read it, and we hadn't needed to discuss it. We both knew what we knew.

We both had felt sure that if anybody came in Friday night, he would come in the same way that he had last night.

He would come in the dining room window, so that he could go up the elevator rather than the stairs, to avoid being seen by a police officer waiting downstairs, which was where the officer yesterday had waited.

He would come up the elevator, and Millner would be ready for him. That was what Millner had planned.

But the killer had other plans, and if the investigating officers hadn't known Captain Millner, the plans might have worked.

The television had apparently been on all night; now it was showing some mindless piece of junk, but I hadn't turned it off yet, for very good reasons. I was glad Jeanne hadn't thought to do it either.

The VCR also was on, but it wasn't showing anything. Presumably it had come to the end of the tape and rewound itself.

"Jeanne, get me some tongs from the kitchen," I said.

She didn't ask why. She went.

Using the tongs to avoid messing up any fingerprints, I pushed the "eject" button and waited for the tape to back itself out. Then, still using the tongs, I lifted the tape out.

*Independence Day.*

A very good movie; though I was somewhat less than delighted by some of its language I loved it otherwise, partly because of its overall themes: not *what can I get out of doing?* but *what can I do?*; not *let's see how many graphic sex scenes we can get into one movie,* but *let's see how many ways we can show the importance of marriage and children;* not *let's throw God out with the bathwater,* but *let's get married in a chapel, let's pray in a crisis.*

I figured Captain Millner would have loved it as much as I did, for the same reasons. Although he neither understood nor approved of my church, he was still a devout family man.

But he would never have watched it or any other movie while he was on stakeout.

I knew, and everybody who had ever worked with him knew, that he'd taught every cop he'd ever worked with that on a stakeout, you don't read a book. You don't turn on the radio. You don't turn on the television. You watch, and you listen, and that is all. Absolutely all.

I didn't know who had killed Captain Millner. I didn't know how. But I did know why.

He was killed for being in the way, just like Sue was.

I'd cry later. Right now I had too much work to do.

# VII

SATURDAY, NOVEMBER 13

# 1

YOU TRY TO SHIFT YOUR EMOTIONS INTO neutral and your brain into warp drive.

While Harry was throwing his clothes on, I had sat down at my computer desk in the numbness of early shock and started making lists of what to do next, so that when I got there I would do them. This is something all cops, or at least all good cops, do regularly, except that usually the lists are in the brain rather than on paper.

As you're patrolling you think, *What would I do if a robbery went down at First Interstate Bank?* And you mentally plot out your routes and your procedures, so that when the day comes that there really *is* a robbery at First Interstate Bank you don't have to stop and think what to do. You already know, and your careful preplanning takes over.

But there are some things that nobody ever preplans. And this was one of them.

"Deb? I'm ready," Harry said.

"Just let me print this out," I answered in what even I heard as a monotone, and I watched as the printer ran. Then, automatically, I closed the paper tray again, so that a cat couldn't jump up on it and break it off, thereby making the printer unusable.

Mechanically, automatically, I turned off the computer and the monitor and then I reached up into that high, awkward position where Harry had put the electrical outlet and the telephone outlet and I unplugged both of them.

We weren't expecting thunderstorms today, and that's the only time the computer needs to be completely unplugged.

But I was on autopilot. I was painting by the numbers right now.

I had still been on autopilot when Harry parked our car in the mass of other cars already in front of the Minot house some two minutes later. When I went past the uniformed officer stationed by the front door, Harry followed me. I didn't stop him; neither did the patrolman, who had managed to find a length of black electrical tape to tape diagonally across his badge.

Harry went with me up the stairs and into Curtis Minot's room.

Yes, the second computer was gone. I scarcely needed to check it to know, but I checked anyway. Then, still in Curtis's room, I called the computer man to tell him not to bother to come in. I caught him just in time, as he was loading his tools into his car preparatory to going out the door.

Then I went into the television room, where Captain Millner still lay on his side, as if he had slumped over from a sitting position.

Harry hadn't touched anything. I didn't need to tell him not to. He'd gone with me to enough crime scenes that he knew the procedure.

Apparently Gary had dressed as fast as I had, and I didn't even want to guess at the speed with which he had driven to get to the Minot house before I had. He hadn't shaved, and he was wearing a gray sweatpants and sweatshirt outfit that said it belonged to Alcatraz. I had seen the catalog which sold that outfit; it was one of those my husband, who is on every militia and survivalist mailing list in the country, gets regularly; but even if I hadn't seen it I would be pretty sure Gary hadn't really stolen the clothes from Alcatraz. He was, after all, a police lieutenant, in charge of both the homicide unit, which I had inhabited for several years, and the major crimes unit, which I presently inhabited. It was alarming sometimes to think how high up the seniority ladder I was by now.

"Sure I wanted a promotion," Gary Hollister said after glancing around just long enough to identify me with Harry right behind me, "but I didn't want it this bad." He was staring at the body, his eyes far redder than his graying red hair.

Like me, he knew what to look for at a crime scene, and he knew Captain Millner. We'd have to wait for the autopsy to know how it was done, but we knew we were looking at murder. And I, at least, whether anybody else agreed or not, suspected that the overturned coffee cup on the end table might hold part of the answer.

I very rapidly lost count of the number of police officers, uniformed and plainclothes, who came to this scene and reluctantly left it again. They weren't all part of the Fort Worth Police Department; officers from other agencies had come in and left, as had a couple of Texas Rangers.

Irene and Bob were downstairs fiddling with the dining room window again; as I expected, they had found it open again. Of course, neither the bypassed alarm wire nor the holes in the window had been fixed yesterday, so all the perp had to do was come right back in the same way. In fact, part of the reason it hadn't been fixed was that we were hoping he *would* come back in the same way.

Nobody from the medical examiner's office had arrived yet.

Kenneth somehow had managed to poke his way in among us. "Did somebody kill that old guy?" he asked me.

"Yes." My voice sounded like a tightwire.

"That was crummy. He talked to me a long time last night, before he told me I had to go to bed. He was a nice old guy. I wish *he* had been my dad."

I turned in some surprise; that was the first favorable word I had heard Kenneth say about anybody. And he meant it: tears were welling up in his eyes, and he turned abruptly and shouldered his way back out.

"Whoever did this—" Dub Arnold's voice was shaking with rage, and he didn't finish the sentence. I hadn't heard him arrive—police officers had been coming and going steadily throughout the hour I'd been here—but now he turned to me. "Deb," he said, "let's leave the work here to Gary. From that message you left for me last night, I gather you and I have some possibles to go and look at."

The FBI, of course, does not have primary jurisdiction on any murder occurring outside of a federally controlled area, unless it is the murder of a federal employee. But in this case, nobody had any doubts that the murder of Captain Millner resulted from his investigation into a crime that was involved with an ongoing federal investigation. The FBI was moving in to continue its ongoing investigation of the relationship between firearms smuggling, Curtis Minot, and Daniel Ellis, and the murder of Curtis Minot had automatically become part of that investigation. Officially, FBI cooperation in the investigation of the murders of Sue Rimer and Scott Millner was purely coincidental.

But Dub was as red-eyed as I was, as Gary was. He'd work this one as hard as any of the rest of us would.

I looked back from Dub to Captain Millner, my throat aching even more. I'd always pretended to hate it when he called me, often at two in the morning, with that "De-e-eb, come to Papa." But I didn't really hate it, and he knew I didn't. It was a game we played.

We had played a lot of games over the years. He'd had ongoing jokes—gentle jokes, not the kind that hurt—with and about everybody he worked with.

I still suspected the solution to this case would be found right under this roof—but who?

The dining room window suggested somebody from the outside, but how had the first entry, when Curtis was killed, been made?

I kept coming back to the alleged fact that the alarm had been turned off when Kenneth entered the house.

I could not imagine any reason whatever for Kenneth to want to kill Captain Millner, or for Jeanne to do it. And there wasn't anybody else here at the right time for all the killings.

Was there?

Then where had the computers gone?

I barely noticed when Harry said, "Will you be okay, babe?"

"Uh-huh," I said.

"You need me to leave you the car?"

"Uh-uh. I'm okay."

Still he hesitated before turning and going down the stairs.

This time the crime scene crew would search the attic and the crawl space under the house, and the interior and the trunk and under the seats of all the vehicles. They'd already searched it all once; they would do it once again now that the captain had been found dead.

They'd search the swimming pool room and the pool itself, with someone going down in a rubberized suit to search the bottom of the pool and all the drains and feeds and so forth.

They'd search the garden shed.

They'd look inside toilet tanks and dismantle the washing machine to look on the outside of its drum. They would pull the refrigerator out from the wall and look in the back of it. They'd look inside and under the dryer and the dishwasher.

They'd look under all the beds and between mattresses and box springs. They'd bring in ladders and look at the backs of all the shelves, even the top ones. They'd pull out all the books and look in, under, and behind them. All the groceries. All the dishes. All the linens.

If there was a place in this house that hadn't already been searched at least twice, I couldn't imagine what it was. And now they were going to search all of it all over again.

They'd found a lot of guns in earlier searches. But not one of them was a .22, and not a one of them showed up on any computer registry of stolen guns; in fact, most of them had legally been imported by Curtis Minot when he still had a federal firearms license.

They'd found a lot of ammunition, but not one round of it was for a .22.

They'd found no drugs, no military hardware, no contraband of any kind.

Now they were going to search everything again, even though they already knew they wouldn't find anything, just in case there was an outside chance that somebody might have put something somewhere they had already searched, figuring that since it was searched before it wouldn't be again. By now three FBI agents had arrived, a federal search warrant had joined our state search warrant, and the Rangers who had come and gone were back again, and so was somebody—I didn't catch his name—from the ATF. Every possible agency was going all out on this one. But going all out often is not enough.

Some crimes are never solved.

I'd cared even when it was Curtis, whom I didn't really know except by sight.

But I'd known Scott Millner about half my life.

# 2

Dub and I did not go right out and start talking to people. We sat down first to share a real breakfast at a cafe while we skimmed through the fat green book, picking out names, addresses, and phone numbers that might do us some good. Then we went to Dub's office, not mine, to do some computer searches to get what background we could get easily. After that, we picked out a few people who looked very interesting.

Four—well, call it five, but two were connected to the same case—looked very promising, partly because Dub recognized the names, having been involved in the cases. There was also Ellis, who was presumably still in Maryland, but Dub had made a phone call to Baltimore requesting a couple of FBI agents to go out and have a word or two with him, particularly in view of Kenneth's polygraph reaction to his name.

The other four—well, I'll list them.

First on our alphabetical list was Nudara Bint Akram Umm Jamil Akhbar, whose husband, Ashraf, had lost his gasoline station and was doing life in prison for murder after being found in possession of two truckloads of hijacked gasoline— that he insisted he didn't know were hijacked until two hours before he was arrested, when Curtis Minot telephoned to let him know both that and the fact that the driver of the second truckload had been shot during the hijacking, and to warn that if he ratted his son Jamil would be murdered.

The FBI, which had primary jurisdiction in this one

because the gasoline trucks were involved in interstate commerce, had looked hard at Ashraf Akhbar from the start, when one of the hijacked trucks was found in a weedy vacant lot directly behind his service station. When his fingerprints, on record from his citizenship application, were found patently visible in the oily black dust on the side of the truck near the master nozzle that is used to pump the gasoline into the underground tank, the FBI looked much harder at Ashraf Akhbar. At this point, of course, the name of Curtis Minot hadn't come into the case.

Akhbar cooperated with the investigation from the start; he told the FBI what Minot, or the man who said he was Minot, threatened, and to his relief nobody followed up on the threat to Jamil. He pointed out that in view of the fact that he'd had to help the driver with the hose, and probably had leaned against the truck at that time, finding his fingerprints there proved nothing at all.

Because Minot was already suspect in a lot of fancy deals, the FBI looked long and hard at him; they'd have been glad to pin him, with or without help from Akhbar, with or without pinning Akhbar. But they couldn't find anything they could prove. A lot of words, yes. But that was all. According to Dub, every FBI agent he'd talked with had agreed: Minot was a smart crook.

Jamil Akhbar, twenty years old, born an American citizen and working on a degree in criminal justice, had sworn in court that his father wouldn't knowingly buy stolen goods and certainly would never have murdered anyone. But the pistol—Russian-made—that had fired the bullet that was found in the dead driver's head turned up in Akhbar's gasoline station, tucked inside the tank of the men's rest room toilet, wrapped in a plastic bag with Akhbar's fingerprints on the inside of it.

Akhbar himself had gone on the stand to explain that he bought the gasoline on the spot market; like most small independent service station owners, he normally dealt in the spot market rather than having standing orders and scheduled delivery dates. The man who'd called to offer him the deal had said he was Curtis Minot, had said he was doing a favor for a friend of a friend who'd produced more gasoline than his regular customers wanted because a couple of his regular customers had suddenly folded. An oil company executive testified that this was not totally unheard of in the market, but it didn't happen often.

Akhbar said that the gasoline was delivered normally except that the tank truck driver—both trucks, which arrived on two successive days, had the same driver—had requested payment in cash, which was rather odd, and had left receipts with no name printed on the form and the signature illegible. Akhbar had been required to go with the driver to the bank to get the money out—the first time, after the gasoline was pumped into the underground tanks; the second time, before it was pumped. But he had to admit that he didn't know the driver; that the driver was not in the courtroom; that he didn't know Curtis Minot except from talking with him by phone, which meant that he had no way whatever of knowing he was really doing business with Minot; and that he couldn't really say from his own knowledge that Minot was involved in any way.

The original driver of one truck was dead; the original driver of the other truck insisted the last thing he saw was an Arab-looking guy, or maybe it was a Hispanic-looking guy, trying to flag him down in the fog, and he stopped because he thought there might be a wreck ahead. He woke up four days later in the hospital. He tentatively identified Akhbar but said he couldn't be sure.

Of course Akhbar couldn't pick out Curtis Minot in court, any more than he could pick out the driver. He said his wife packed his lunch every day in plastic bags like that, and he probably left his fingerprints inside the bag while getting his food out, and after he ate his lunch he threw the bag in the trash, from whence anyone could have picked it up. As to the rest room, it wasn't kept locked, and plenty of people used it;

how was he supposed to know how the plastic bag with the pistol in it got into the toilet tank? He had no reason to notice anybody using the rest room any more than he noticed anybody else using the rest room, particularly since the rest rooms were around the side of the building. And anyway, did anybody really think that if he'd committed the hijackings and murder he'd have been so stupid as to park the truck behind his service station and put the gun in the toilet tank?

All these things, as well as his furious insistence that his very name, Ashraf, meant "honor," meant nothing to the jury. *Arab* and *terrorist* are too closely hooked together in the American mind.

The FBI, which suspected Akhbar was telling the truth, recommended leniency to the court.

Akhbar didn't get leniency.

Bran Caley, who took delivery in Ireland of the shipload of rifles he'd spent IRA money to buy in Fort Worth only to find half of them too rusty to use, was next in alphabetical order, but I wanted to go see him first for a lot of reasons. He was the only one that we knew for a fact had recently threatened Minot—and now we also knew for a fact that he had no legal right to be in the United States at all. He was a known IRA terrorist. He'd sullenly pled *nolo contendere*, which is legalese for "I'm not going to tell you whether I did it or not and I'm not going to argue about it, so just sentence me and get it over with," and had refused to say anything else, either when he was charged or when he was sentenced. He hadn't named Curtis Minot as the source of the weapons he'd been caught trying to smuggle out of the United States. He hadn't named anybody. He hadn't said anything. And he'd been deported, forbidden to return, and promised hard time in a federal prison if he did return. Finding his name and address in Minot's notebook was the first anybody in the FBI even suspected of a connection between Minot and Caley.

Dub told me that Santiago Ramirez, who was next on the list, would have been deported, in his case to Bolivia, as soon as he was out of prison, which shouldn't have been very soon in view of the fact that he had been sentenced to ten to twenty for smuggling. But that meant he might do four or five. Sentences are a joke, for the most part. Customs believed he had been laundering cocaine money through Minot; at least one customs official suspected that Minot had kept the last batch of money and possibly had been the snitch that helped catch Ramirez at the border bringing in the next load of cocaine. During his trial, Ramirez had breathed a lot of threats against Minot.

The U.S. Customs Service and the FBI, on the basis of Ramirez's sworn testimony as well as on allegations from other sources, looked very hard at Minot, but there never was enough to put him away. He had legal businesses that accounted for all his large income, and he'd properly paid taxes on it and hadn't been spending above it.

Dub said that, like Caley, if Ramirez was presently in the United States as Curtis's records indicated both were, he was illegal. All the computer had told us was that he was no longer in prison. That, we learned later, was accurate as far as it went, but it didn't tell the whole story.

Dan Sutherland, whose father, Ross Sutherland, had died in poverty after discovering that the twenty acres of oil land he'd counted on to make him comfortable in his retirement had no oil left as a result of somebody's slant-well drilling, was another possibility. I had to explain to Dub what slant-well drilling was. There'd been a major scandal about it when I was just a kid: somebody would lease the oil rights to land which in fact did not have any oil but was adjacent to land which did have oil. Then, instead of drilling straight down, the well-drillers would drill at a lowering slant, tapping the oil under the adjacent land, thus turning over to the owner of the mineral rights of the adjoining land the royalties which should have gone to the owner of the mineral rights of the land under which the oil actually was located. The mineral rights owner is not necessarily the owner of the surface of the land; that confusion, along with a good many others—including the fact that Texas, unlike all other states of the union, has sea and undersea rights clear out to the national limit—is a result of some of the clauses of the joint resolution of Congress under which the Republic of Texas had become a part of the United States. (Though the resolution has always been regarded as a treaty, it's actually not one because President Tyler couldn't get the necessary two-thirds majority in both houses necessary to ratify the treaty; some exponents of international law still insist the annexation of Texas was illegal as a result of the way it was done.)

In slant-drilling, land chicanery usually preceded the drilling, so that the mineral profits went to the figurehead mineral rights owner and fed back from there into the company doing the slant-drilling.

When Ross Sutherland, already seriously ill with lung cancer, learned that the oil under his land was gone, he had called every state and federal agency he could think of, insisting that Minot was behind the slant-drilling. The state managed to cobble up a case of sorts—that was Minot's only arrest—but Minot convinced the jury that the whole thing was an accident; obviously he didn't drill the well himself, though he admitted to owning both the mineral rights for the land on which the well was dug and the company that did the drilling, and he didn't know why the driller, who was conveniently dead, had drilled into the adjoining land. By that time the oil was gone, Minot's oil company had gone out of business, and only skimpy records remained; Minot, of course, walked.

By the time that case went to trial Ross Sutherland was dead, and his son Dan had more than a few times then and since then been heard to say *somebody* ought to kill Minot. But there was no evidence that he'd decided to take on the job himself.

There were others. The little green address book was bristling with names of people who had reasons to hate Curtis Minot. But we decided to start with these. "I want to just look at them to start with," I told Dub. "Never mind warrants; I want to get a feel for the people. We can go back later with warrants."

"That's fine except for Caley and Ramirez," Dub agreed. "And I don't know how current his address for Ramirez is, because Ramirez ought to be out of the country. If we even knock on their doors we've got to go in loaded for bear." By "loaded for bear" this time he didn't mean firearms; he meant arrest and search warrants.

"Well, yeah, that's true," I agreed, "and if we're getting warrants anyway, then I guess we might as well get search warrants for all of the others just in case. That way we don't have to come back in to get one if—uh—"

"If there are complications," Dub said delicately.

So we started by getting federal search warrants and, in the case of Caley and Ramirez, federal arrest warrants.

That meant we had to give probable cause for asking for each of those search warrants.

And even though the judge was certainly on our side, we still had to come up with probable cause sufficient for a federal court. This took somewhat more than the additional half-hour or so we'd hoped to spend in Dub's office.

# 3

WHEN YOU KNOCK ON THE DOOR OF A known terrorist, you never know what to expect.

It was a very small apartment, one of six apparently converted from old-fashioned cabin-style motor inns that preceded the creation of motels by the hundreds on every highway. I covered the front, Dub covered the back, and I knocked on the door with my left hand because my pistol was in my right hand.

"Who is it?" asked a richly accented voice from inside, but the man was opening the door as he asked it, and I got a good look at bare feet, wrinkled and dirty khaki chino trousers, and a not very clean vest-style undershirt before I ever saw his unshaven face. When he saw me, complete with pistol and warrant, he cursed once, loudly, but he showed no sign whatever of fight. He just raised his hands and said, "What now?"

"Deb Ralston, Fort Worth Police Department," I said. "May I come in?"

"You might as well." He turned away from the door and I followed, watching him closely, because this kind of show of compliance sometimes is followed by a lightning snatch at a concealed weapon. But he didn't grab for anything; he just sat down on the couch and said, "You want to handcuff me or something? I'm tired of my hands in the air."

"Not at the moment," I said. "You can rest your hands on the top of your head. I've got an FBI agent with me. May he come in?"

The man shrugged as well as he could with his fingers locked together on top of his head. "Might as well. How about turning the telly off?" He nodded toward the television, which was on and loud.

Dub came in through the back door, which apparently had been left unlocked, and displayed his identification. "Are you Bran Caley?" he asked after I turned the television off.

"Yeah, you've got me."

"What does that mean?" Dub asked.

"Yeah, I'm Bran Caley. Anything else you want to know?"

"You have the right to remain silent—"

"Just hand it over," Caley said. "I'll sign it. I've no reason not to."

It was Dub who decided, for Caley's safety as well as our own, that we'd better handcuff him, but after I checked the cushions and down behind and between them to make sure there was no convenient weaponry there, Dub handcuffed him with his hands in front of him. For now, at least, he was co-operating.

Bran Caley was, to quote an old phrase, "black Irish." That meant he had wavy coal-black hair, brown eyes, and very fair skin. Yes, he was in the IRA, or at least part of it; it now (and probably always) has several parts that often do not coordinate well if at all with one another. Yes, he'd been deported from the United States as part of a suspended sentence for violation of firearms purchase and export laws. Yes, he'd returned illegally, and yes, he knew he was probably headed for federal prison in Atlanta.

None of that seemed to bother him very much.

In particular, the death of Curtis Minot didn't bother him very much; he already knew about it, as it had been all over the newspapers and television, and he'd halfway had a hunch that somebody might come looking for him about it. Yes, he'd quarreled with Minot, and he wasn't surprised we'd been told.

"My only complaint is that I didn't get a chance to pull the trigger," he said. "Or maybe kick him around a few times beforehand." I was fascinated to notice how much his accent sounded like that of *Deep Space Nine*'s Chief O'Brian.

"This is a search warrant," Dub began. "It entitles us to—"

Caley dropped his head into his hands and interrupted, "Must I listen to that again? All roight, all roight, all roight, give it here. What difference does it make? I'm out of things to lose." (Fleetingly I thought of an old country song that describes freedom as meaning "nothing left to lose." That wasn't a kind of freedom I'd want.) "My wife died four years ago when somebody blew up a Catholic pub where she worked. I've got no kids. And I'm not even any use now to the IRA, not when I'm known this well. You want to know about Curtis Minot? Let me tell you about Curtis Minot." He sat back on his couch, handcuffed hands up and propping the back of his head, feet sprawled out in front of him.

"That quarrel your informer told you about—how shall I begin? This was the third time we'd bought from Minot. The first couple of times, no problem, but they were small purchases: a hundred shoulder-to-air missiles one time, a couple of hundred Glock 17s." (I didn't consider one hundred shoulder-to-air missiles or two hundred military-style full-automatic pistols to be small stuff.) "This last time we went bigger: we trusted him by then, and he said he had gotten hold of a thousand BARs—the M1918A1, the one with a bipod, .30 caliber. Six hundred rounds a minute. He said he had a thousand of them, and six hundred thousand rounds of ammo still wrapped in oil paper, never used. He'd let us have them for a hundred dollars apiece for the rifles, ten cents per round for the ammo. Don't bother to add it up, it comes to 160,000 dollars. Shipping was extra. He said that price was cheap. And it would have been, especially the ammo, if he'd shipped what he sold.

"He wanted the money in advance. That kind of thing, they usually do. It was hard to scratch up, but we got it, and in due time the shipment arrived."

I was so interested in his accent I almost didn't notice what he was saying, but I didn't quite not notice. If this had something to do with Captain Millner's death—

"Well, when we opened the boxes we found out about four hundred rifles were in good shape. Another two hundred maybe could be cleaned up good enough to use. The rest were so rusted they weren't fit even for fenceposts. And the ammo? It wasn't new. It had been reloaded so many times some of the cartridges were split right down the side. One exploded in a rifle I was firing."

Having had that happen to me one year on the police target range when I was doing my annual qualifying, I could certainly sympathize with him on that matter. I was firing a pistol, using often-reloaded wadcutters, and the explosion jerked my hand to the side, severely spraining my wrist. Fortunately it didn't harm my pistol. Unlike wrists, pistols don't heal on their own, and I was pretty broke at the time. It was after Harry got out of the Marines, but before he went to work at Bell Helicopter.

"So I came back here about a year ago to discuss the matter with him. Somebody told him I was coming, and he set me up—real good, he set me up. Those arms I was caught with, I didn't buy. They were planted on me. Your government didn't send me to prison that time; they just deported me, but they said they'd send me to prison if I came back.

"Well, I came back anyway, having as you might say a bone to pick with Curtis Minot, and I got forty thousand dollars out of him—under a fourth of what we spent, counting shipping." (So I was probably right that the nest egg in the safe had once been a round five hundred thousand dollars.) "He laughed a lot about it. He said it was fair, half the guns were good, all the ammo was good, he kept three-fourths of the money. Half the guns weren't good. And none of the ammo could be trusted. I stayed here trying to find more weapons; I didn't expect to be caught. Obviously." He shrugged. "I suppose I'll go to prison. It's a roight cop, you got me fair and square. But if I have to go I'm glad somebody took care of Curtis Minot first."

His eyes, which had been on Dub, switched to me. "Somebody offed your captain? I'm sorry. I know how that feels. The blasted Brits offed my captain."

With this sympathy from so unexpected a source, I could feel tears welling up in my eyes again. I nodded, and Dub glanced at me. "You okay, Deb?"

"Yeah, sure," I got out, and Dub returned his attention to Caley.

"How did you know that?" he asked.

Caley nodded toward the television again. "It's been all over the telly. Minot offed on Thursday, your Captain Millner offed today. At Minot's house. I'd be a fool not to see the connection. And I'm no fool."

"So what went with the money?" Dub asked.

"What money?"

"The money Minot refunded to you."

This time Caley actually laughed, eyes sparkling with brief but real humor. "In your dreams, man, in your dreams!"

Dub looked at me. "If I offer a deal, how do you feel about it?"

"If he doesn't know anything about the murders, I'll back you," I said.

"Caley," Dub said, "I'm in the mood to be friendly. You tell me more about Minot and get that money back as evidence, and I'll look the other way while you walk out that door, as long as you first promise me that you'll leave this country on the first available transportation and never come back."

"No deal," Caley said. "I've told you all I know about Minot. If I knew any more I'd tell you. But the rest of it—no deal."

"You'd rather go to prison?"

"I'd rather go to prison."

"I'm trying to be fair," Dub said.

Caley shrugged. "No deal," he said again, and started whistling "Kevin Barry," which, as I know the words, gave me a pretty fair idea how his mind was working. The song is about an Irish rebel, a teenage boy, who chooses to be hanged rather than turn informer. Caley must have been able to tell from my face that I recognized the song, because, looking straight at me with his eyes twinkling slightly again, he softly sang a couple of lines as they are in one of the several versions:

> Turn informer and we'll free you;
> Kevin Barry answered no.

Then he stopped whistling.

Dub walked over to the telephone and called the federal marshal's office to come pick up the federal prisoner. Certainly *we* had no intention of making the arrest. We were busy.

# 4

$H$E DIDN'T DO IT," I SAID TO DUB TWO hours later.

Caley had departed in handcuffs half an hour earlier, and we'd searched the entire apartment very thoroughly. It was small and there wasn't much in it; we could have searched it reasonably thoroughly in twenty minutes, but the IRA is known to be canny— They've smuggled guns and ammo inside the diapers of babies and inside corpses being sent home for burial. With that in mind, we'd tried every place we could think of, including the undersides of dresser drawers and the insides of curtain rods, the attic (such as it was) and the crawl space (which was even worse), as well as standard places such as toilet tanks and closet shelves. Caley had just watched us, looking amused, until he was taken away.

"I know he didn't do it," Dub agreed. "But we had to look. I'm interested now in this Akhbar fellow. But before we go anywhere else, I want to check in with my office." He reached for the telephone.

He hung it up some minutes later and turned to me. "Daniel Ellis isn't in Maryland," he told me. "Daniel Ellis is in Fort Worth."

"You've got the address?"

"I've got the address."

The velocity with which the two of us departed Bran Caley's small apartment and headed for Dub's car irresistibly reminded me of certain scenes in *The X-Files*.

# 5

---

**I**T WAS THE OTHER END OF THE SCALE FROM where Caley had been: an apartment-hotel, with the kind of suites that are often leased long-range by large businesses to house trainees and visiting VIPs, and I'd guess that a month's worth of rental charges on those suites would be about the same as six months' worth of my house payments, if not more.

The resident manager was not pleased to give us Daniel Ellis's suite number. He did it anyway rather than insisting we return with a warrant, because he was impressed by the FBI identification card. He even let it slip out, deliberately or otherwise, that Ellis had a permanent suite there for the use of his sources and customers as well as himself. It was never rented out to anybody else. And the apartments were more expensive than I had thought. If you rented by the day, you'd pay—per day—as much as my monthly house payment.

Ellis didn't rent by the day. He rented by the year. Which told us Ellis wasn't short of money.

Of course the manager didn't give us a key. We wouldn't have accepted it if he had done so. We didn't have a search warrant for Daniel Ellis, and we didn't have any probable cause to get one. At this point, all we wanted to do was talk with him.

For all the good *that* did us. Ellis apparently wasn't there, or at least he didn't answer his door or his telephone—Dub, using his cellular phone, tried to telephone into the apartment from just outside its door.

"What next?" I asked as I slammed the passenger's side door and Dub slid under the steering wheel.

"How he got here might be interesting," Dub answered.

"Here meaning Fort Worth, or this place?"

"Fort Worth," Dub said. "Thing is, his wife apparently thinks he's legit. So she didn't have any reason to keep secrets. And one of the things she told our agent was, Ellis flew to Fort Worth."

"So?"

"Not commercial. He has a private plane."

That was interesting but not very. Lots of people have private planes. Harry had one until last year: twenty-five years ago he and five other men went in on it together, and one by one the other men got bored and Harry bought their shares. The last ten years that it sat in the hangar (that we had to pay rent on, twelve months of the year) he flew it exactly four times. Even so, I was astonished when finally, and voluntarily, he sold it.

I was not surprised when he spent the money he got from the sale on a videocamera good enough for a television station and on a bigger and better computer system. Harry is fond of his toys, which is why the maze of small rooms that used to be our garage is half-full of things like CB radios, ham radios, model trains, a small kiln for melting lead to reload shotgun shells at home (no longer used since, with some prodding from me, he decided that keeping quantities of gunpowder at home was not the world's safest thing to do), and various other items more or less abandoned from the time he fell in love with the next toy.

I wasn't holding my breath for him to get rid of the computer. We now had three. Harry had reluctantly moved his new one out of the living room and into another of the small rooms in the garage, which he outfitted with lights, electrical and telephone outlets, and enough other paraphernalia to stock at least two Radio Shack stores. When he bought his new computer he gave the old one to Lori, with the offhand explanation that of course she and Hal, when Hal got home from his mission, would need it, and in the meantime Lori could use it for school (she couldn't possibly continue to use either his or mine, as she had been doing all along). Yes, of course I had one all my own, no matter how little use I had for it: while we were in Utah a year ago, taking Hal to the MTC, Harry had bought a secondhand computer for me; that one lived in the bedroom, where I used it to make out grocery lists, read on-line magazines (once in a blue moon when I had time), do the ward newsletter (which was now down to once a year, due to Church budget cuts), and play an occasional computer game.

I had deleted a good many of the computer games that either came with the computer or were added to it later either by its first owner—now dead—or Harry. This startled Harry, because he knew that I had been playing one game, called Midnight Oil, with considerable avidity because it was the one solitaire game I'd ever seen that depends on skill rather than luck. It had taken me three months of frustration to learn how to do it well, but ever since then my cumulative score had been steadily rising. When last checked, it was up to 78.52, meaning that I had won 78.52 percent of all the games I had played. I was aiming for eighty when I took the plunge and deleted the game.

"Why'd you do that?" asked Harry. "You were getting so good at it."

I answered, "How much good does it do to get good at something that's not worth doing anyway?"

He had no answer to that.

I brought my mind back to the present, as Dub turned off the Old Denton Highway to head for the small private airport I was quite familiar with because it's the one that once housed Harry's plane. It was the one where the man who framed my son-in-law Olead Baker—of course, he wasn't my son-in-law then—for murder, had kept his plane.

We wandered around and looked around.

We didn't have a search warrant, so we couldn't open the

plane; the best we could do, even if we did figure out which one it was (which I wasn't betting on) would be to look through the windows.

After a while a man came and asked us who we were and what we were doing, and Dub told him who we were and what we were doing. "Oh yeah, Ellis," he said. "That's his over there."

It was a Piper Cub.

Anybody who could afford the hotel-apartment space Ellis was renting could afford something a lot bigger than a Piper Cub, which Harry insists is a toy airplane. But different people like different things. "Does he keep a car out here when he's not in town?" Dub asked casually.

Responding to the casual tone as Dub had meant him to, the man said, "Oh yeah, he's got this dark blue Bronco. It's not here now, though. He's gone in it. He pays for the space. When the plane is here the car is gone; when the car is here the plane is gone."

"Makes sense," Dub agreed.

"You all need any more?" the man asked.

"No, you've been real helpful," Dub said.

The man looked at me quizzically. "Now you, lady, I've seen you before. Who are you?"

"Harry Ralston's wife."

"Oh, yeah, yeah, yeah, I remember. The one that's a cop."

"Right," I said, wondering if the man thought Harry had several wives so that "the one that's a cop" had to be defined so thoroughly.

"Well, I guess I better get to work," the man said, and didn't. He continued to stand and watch us hopefully as we walked toward the plane and looked in the windows.

What looked like a junior high school textbook was open on the passenger's seat. *Well, so what,* I thought for a moment; *we know Ellis has a junior high school son.*

But then I looked more closely. The name written inside the textbook was not Ellis.

It was Kenneth Minot.

So Kenneth had hitchhiked home. Sure he did. But by air. And apparently Daniel Ellis had been in Fort Worth as long as Kenneth Minot had.

That was extremely interesting, and I would have to ponder at considerable length on its meaning.

We were leaving the hangar building, heading for Dub's car, when Dub's cellular phone sounded. He answered and then handed it to me.

"Deb," said Gary Hollister, "isn't this your day off?"

"Yes, but—"

He sounded as weary as I felt. "Scott"—unlike me, Gary had called Captain Millner by his first name—"told me that when I took over his job I'd have a problem with you. You never know when to quit, and you don't take care of your health. Go home *right now*. Don't try to do any more work until Monday unless you have a direct order from me to do so, and if dispatch or anybody else calls you tell them what I said and don't go unless you hear from me. And don't try to just go and visit your friend Jeanne. We've got four officers staked out now and they or their replacements will be there for at least the next week. *Get some rest.* By the way, are you about ready to be a lieutenant?"

"No." That was an immediate, knee-jerk reaction, and Gary saw it as such.

"That's too bad," he said, "because Scott and I had already discussed it with the chief. I'm taking Scott's place, and that means my spot is open and we need somebody in it. Somebody good. So think it over and see if you can come up with a better answer. The funeral's Thursday—"

"Why so late?" I interrupted.

"Because the ME's office has to wait for preliminary toxicology reports before releasing the body."

The body. A thing. Not a person any longer. Part of the *corpus delecti*, the body of the crime. Not a person we knew and loved and worked and laughed and cried with. This is the worst thing about police work—not danger, not nastiness, not even the sewer rats we have to talk to every day, but the need to depersonalize. If we couldn't do it we couldn't work. But it's a hard pose to maintain when "the body" is that of a friend.

There wasn't a single person in the medical examiner's office who didn't know Captain Millner. I couldn't help wondering who did the autopsy—and, even more, *how* whoever it was did it.

Gary had relocated his voice, which broke at the end of his last sentence. He added, "Thursday's plenty of time for you to get your lieutenant's insignia pinned onto your uniform."

I was pretty sure I wouldn't come up with a different answer, but I agreed to think it over. And yes, I would be in uniform for the funeral, even though I hadn't worked in uniform for more than fifteen years, because a police funeral is a pretty ceremonial affair. As to whether I'd be wearing lieutenant's bars by Thursday—well, I doubted it. I doubted it a whole lot.

I didn't have my car. Harry had driven me to Jeanne's house and then I had left with Dub.

Dub drove me home, stopping on the way for me to pick up Cameron, who was mightily pleased by getting a ride home from the FBI and at once began to ask Dub about *The X-Files*, of which Dub, not to my surprise, denied any knowledge.

Just as he pulled up in front of my house, Dub said, "Your boss didn't call *me* off."

"That's right," I said. "So what are you going to do?"

"Go on looking."

"Be careful, will you, Dub?" I said. "I can't spare any more friends this week." I meant my voice to sound light and cheerful, but of course it broke on the last word.

Dub's fingers on the steering wheel tightened, and he said "Yeah" in a voice that was breaking as much as mine was. He cleared his throat, found his voice, and said, "I'm going to run records checks on every name in that diary. And I'll just see what else I can turn up."

When Harry came home, having stopped by the day-care

center under the assumption that I wouldn't have done so, he had pizza with him. That would have been nice if I hadn't already made supper.

Oh well, we could always eat cold (or nuked) pizza the next day.

It wasn't until after Cameron went to bed, after Lori came in and did her homework and went to bed, that I started crying, in a chair in the living room, with my knees drawn up to my chin, as some nameless (to me) comic told stupid (to me) jokes on a television show I never watch.

Harry moved me from the chair to the couch so he could hold me. He was crying too; he hadn't worked with Scott Millner, hadn't known him the way I did, but what he'd known of him he'd liked.

I don't know how long I cried.

It wasn't long enough.

# VIII

Sᴜɴᴅᴀʏ, Nᴏᴠᴇᴍʙᴇʀ 14

# 1

THE NEXT SURPRISE—A GOOD ONE, JUST for a change—occurred immediately after breakfast on Sunday—well, brunch really, because right now our ward was meeting at eleven in the morning. I had made muffins, and Cameron as usual had made a lot of crumbs. I might not have gone to church myself, because I still had considerable tendency to cloud up at odd moments when memories of Captain Millner came into my mind.

I knew that Captain Millner was all right. He was just dead, and on Thursday we'd be burying the body he used to live in. Wherever he was, I had no doubt he was busy and happy. But he'd gone on a very long journey, and those of us left behind were missing him.

But while I was stacking the dishes in the sink and washing the table while Lori was washing Cameron, Harry came out into the kitchen. He does not do this often. Our kitchen is emphatically a one-person kitchen, and sometimes I think it is a no-person kitchen. But here he was, blocking the path into the dining area.

He had shaved.

This might not be such a momentous occasion, except for one thing: Harry does not shave on the weekend. On the weekend Harry seems to work very hard at looking as scroungy as humanly possible: he wears old (like twenty-five years) Marine Corps fatigues, now paint-spattered; he does not shave; he does not comb his hair. His sole concession to normal humanity is that he does brush his teeth. I think he does that only because he knows how close he could not get to me if he didn't.

"What are you doing?" I inquired in pardonable surprise.

"Going to church with you," he answered. "That is okay, isn't it?"

Of course it was okay. Harry is still nominally a Baptist, but the truth is that except for obligatory appearances at weddings and funerals, he has very rarely darkened a church door in the last twenty years. He'd been to sacrament meeting with the rest of the family exactly twice—once for Hal's missionary farewell and once in Salt Lake City the Sunday before we delivered Hal to the MTC on Friday. So to say that I was pleased by this development would be a severe understatement. Pleased? I was overjoyed. And, obviously, now I was definitely going to church, not dropping the least hint to Harry that I had thought of staying home.

He sat attentively through sacrament meeting, which rather surprised me considering that a member of the stake high council was speaking; then he asked me, "What's next?"

"Well, Sunday School," I said, "and then for me, Relief Society. Men go to priesthood meeting, but I don't know whether you would or not."

"Why not?"

"Because you're not a priesthood holder," I tried to explain. The matter of being a priesthood holder had been semi-explained to him before, but he thought that the idea of anyone making our scatterbrained son Hal a priest was so totally absurd that he hadn't paid much attention.

"I see," he said, and turned abruptly to corner the bishop, who in the secular world was Sergeant Will Linden, Fort Worth Police Department. "Is there a time I could talk with you?" he asked.

"Sure," Will said amiably. "Right now, if you'd like."

Sunday School that day will forever remain a blur in my mind; I didn't even know what was being discussed, as I spent

the time alternately thinking about the vast hole Scott Millner's departure had left in my life and frantically wondering
what Harry and the bishop were talking about and how it was
going to affect the entire family. I did manage to listen to the
Relief Society lesson, though, because it was about the importance of sealings, which was a topic very much on my mind
lately. I thought, sitting on the back row and crying quietly,
that nobody would notice, but one of the sisters came and put
her arm around me and gave me a handkerchief, and finally I
stopped crying again. Then she hugged me and said, "Me
too."

When I got out of Relief Society the bishop's door was still
closed, and Harry was nowhere in sight. After retrieving
Cameron from Primary I sat down in the foyer to wait, and
after a while longer Harry emerged rattling his car keys.

"That was a long conversation," I said.

"It was, wasn't it?" Harry replied. That seemed to be all he
had to say. He did not discuss the conversation. I judged it best
not to ask; whatever had happened, he'd tell me when he was
ready to tell me.

Fifteen minutes later, right in the middle of the trip home,
he said, "I know now what you were crying about the other
day."

"Which other day?" I asked. I'd been doing a lot of crying
lately, for very good reasons; I thought I knew which day he
meant, but I wasn't totally sure.

"Right after Curtis was shot. When you were getting ready
to go to court."

"Oh," I said. I remembered that quite well. "So?"

"What?" Cameron demanded, unfastening his seat belt so
that he could lean into the front seat.

"Put your seat belt right back on," Harry said, "and sit
down right. This discussion doesn't concern you."

Actually it did, very much, but not in any way a five-year-
old, or at least this five-year-old, was likely to understand. I
think Lori knew, or guessed, what we were talking about,

though. At any rate, she unbuckled her own seat belt long enough to grab Cameron and firmly set him down. Reluctantly he refastened his seat belt, and she scooted back into her own seat and refastened her own seat belt.

"So I've got to think about it, that's all," Harry said. "I mean, you could have told me about sealings a long time ago." I didn't say anything; he didn't either for a moment. Then he added, "Okay, I know, you tried and Hal tried and I wouldn't listen. But I've got to think."

To say that Hal had tried was something of an understatement. I still vividly remembered one day when Hal was fifteen. Despite his usual boisterous high spirits, the idea of actually getting up in front of anybody to speak terrified him, at least when it was something that mattered; he had dropped out of a junior high speech class when he found out that he was expected to make several three-minute speeches to all of twenty people, all of them friends or at least acquaintances, although he was quite capable of getting up on top of a table in the cafeteria and pretending, very loudly, to be a Klingon warrior.

But all the same he'd come home from school one day, gone into his room for a while (no rock music, no fantasy novels), and then when Harry got home and was lying down for a brief snooze, Hal—white around the mouth from sheer nerves—took a paperbound copy of the Book of Mormon into our room, bore his testimony in a very shaky voice, and then added, "Dad, if you'd ever start going to church with us you'd want to get baptized, and if you got baptized you'd be a bishop in five years."

"Why did you say that?" I'd asked Hal later that evening.

"I don't know," he said. "I think I didn't say it. I think it said itself."

This gave me a lot to think about. But the years rolled on, and Hal turned sixteen, seventeen, eighteen, nineteen, and left on his mission, all with Harry evidencing not the least interest in the Church or even in the paperback Book of Mormon, which had gathered dust on top of his dresser between the times that, in the course of cleaning the room, I dusted it. Finally, about four years ago I put it in Harry's top drawer with his handkerchiefs, equally unused, and I tried to quit thinking about that day very often.

I had tried to quit thinking about my patriarchal blessing, which promised the completion of all family sealings, along with many other blessings, including rising with my loved ones in the first resurrection, if I would do what I knew I should do. But of course I couldn't quit thinking about any of those things; in fact, for the last year I had carried a photocopy of my patriarchal blessing around in my billfold to read whenever I felt really down.

I did the best I could to do what I knew I should do. But Harry remained uninterested, and so did our daughters Vicky and Becky.

I didn't see how any of it was ever going to work out. Maybe in the Millennium? One of my friends told me something her son-in-law said: Eternity is fine; it's time that's the hard part.

But without my husband, without most of my posterity, I wasn't sure how much I was going to like eternity. Time was complicated enough, and it was all I could do to keep track of things I had to do.

Hal was the only one of my children who was a member of the Church; Cameron was a child of record, but he was three years short of being baptized. And even Hal and Cameron couldn't be sealed to me as parent until I was first sealed to my husband. Vicky and her husband, Don, weren't churchgoers at all; Becky and her husband, Olead, were still Baptists, as was my mother.

*Quit fretting, Deb,* I told myself. *Things happen when it's time for them to happen, and not one moment before.*

Of course I didn't quit fretting. How often do I follow the good advice I give myself?

When we arrived home about a quarter to three, after

fifteen minutes of silence, Kenneth Minot was sitting inside our fence on the front doorstep, with one arm around Pat. He wasn't wearing a jacket, and he looked cold. He stood up as we got out of the car. "Where were you so long?" he asked accusingly. "Were you at church?"

"Yes, we were," Harry said, staring at him. Then I realized Harry either hadn't seen him at all at Jeanne's house or hadn't known who he was.

But before I could get my mouth open, Kenneth said, "You sure do stay at church a long time."

"It starts late," I answered, and made the introductions.

Kenneth said a round of "Hi" rather absently, and then said, "Mrs. Ralston, can I talk with you?"

# 2

TALKING WITH A MINOR IN THE ABSENCE OF his parents can be a little tricky. But in this case the minor's father was dead, his mother was a possible suspect, and whose permission was I supposed to get? Surely even Gary would understand that if Kenneth came to me I really did have to talk with him, whether I was on duty or not.

As soon as she had realized what was going on, Lori corralled Cameron and took him to visit Vicky's children. Harry went on into the bedroom, ostensibly for a nap (though I noticed he took my Book of Mormon with him; apparently he'd forgotten he had one of his own), but mainly to stay out of the way in hopes that Kenneth would talk more freely, and to listen in case I needed any help.

I didn't expect to need any help. But you never know.

Kenneth, now sitting in a chair in my living room, looked angry, belligerent, and scared. Now that he had my attention, he didn't seem to know what to do with it. In my house, he looked even skinnier than I remembered him being; his dark hair, curly as his mother's, accented the pallor of his face, and the bruised look under his eyes told me he hadn't had enough sleep lately. The bulky sweater he was wearing in lieu of a jacket only served to demonstrate his small, frail wrists.

"What would you like to talk about?" I asked.

"What do you think I want to talk about?" he demanded.

As the answer to that question was self-evident and he knew it as well as I did, I sat and waited.

It took five minutes, by the clock I could see and he couldn't, before he decided to speak again. When he did, what he said had nothing directly to do with the case. "I wish my house looked like this," he said, looking around the living room.

In some considerable surprise, I also looked around the living room—small, it had always been too small, though not as bad as the kitchen. It could hold five people in something halfway approaching comfort, if none of them were very large people. I tried to figure out why Kenneth would prefer it to the simple elegance of his own living room. The newspaper, which Harry had started but not finished reading before brunch, was scattered about the coffee table, couch, and floor. All the unpaid bills were in a dish on the coffee table, theoretically so that we would see them and remember to pay them, and usually we did unless we were both too preoccupied to think about them or unless Cameron took them away to play with.

There were Kleenex tissues all over the floor; Ivory had lately developed a habit of stealing them out of trash cans or even pulling them out of the box with his teeth, chewing on them for a while, and then leaving them (often in shreds) wherever he happened to drop them, and everybody in the family was used to collecting tissues from the floor and putting them in the closed garbage can in the dining room (no, of course it wasn't in the kitchen; anybody who could get a garbage can into my kitchen could park a Mack truck inside a Volkswagen). We had absentmindedly left Ivory inside the house when we went to church, and nobody yet had collected the current crop of tissues.

The television, positioned on a small cart, was set so that it could be turned to face either the living room or the dining room. One of Cameron's red sneakers was on top of it; the other was on the raised hearth, along with an assortment of Legos with which Cameron had been building a mighty truck (I knew what it was because he had told me; otherwise I'd never have guessed). Lori's math book was on the coffee table over some of the newspapers and under some more of them, which told me she'd been trying to study in the living room while Harry read newspapers, Cameron built a mighty truck, and I made muffins.

But then suddenly I could see it through Kenneth's eyes.

It needed to be tidied, definitely. But you could tell by looking that somebody lived there.

And in Kenneth's house, most of the time you couldn't.

But he didn't come over here to discuss my house. I said, "I'm glad you like it; your house is really much nicer, though."

He glared at me. He knew as well as I did what I meant by that, and he knew I knew what he had meant.

We waited a while longer, each waiting for the other to speak first, before he began to approach what was apparently the object of his visit. "Mr. Ellis called me a while ago and told me you went yesterday and looked at his airplane."

"That's correct. I did." Presumably the man we'd talked with at the airstrip was one of Ellis's information sources. I had rather expected that he was.

"Who was the guy with you? Mr. Ellis said he thought it was an FBI agent. I mean, that's what the guy at the airport told him."

"Yes, the man with me was an FBI agent. His name is William Arnold, and his nickname is Dub."

Kenneth sat a while longer, alternately wiggling and fidgeting. He was sitting in Harry's chair, which made him look more than ever like a very small child. No, there was no way he'd ever make the breadth of shoulder of his father, or his height, or his body build. His looks? Or Jeanne's? Well, Jeanne's maybe, if he ever looked happy. From what I had heard from Jeanne and from him, I wasn't sure he ever did look happy.

"I know *The X-Files* isn't true," he blurted. "But is there anything like that really?"

Why does everybody want to discuss *The X-Files* with me every time I mention the FBI? I rarely even watch it, though

Harry is taping every episode so that when Hal gets home from his mission he can catch up on the whole storyline, in what will presumably be a week or longer orgy of television watching.

"I don't think so," I said. "If there is, Dub doesn't know anything about it, or at least he hasn't told me. Was that what you wanted to talk about?"

Kenneth didn't answer. He looked at his hands. He looked at his fingernails. He looked at the floor. He looked at the cocker spaniel, who was in the process of trying to get in his lap, but his lap was somewhat smaller than the cocker spaniel. He looked everywhere except at me.

Ivory managed to get up, with about a third of his body including his head in Kenneth's lap and the rest sprawled about the rest of the chair. Harry has a large chair, and Kenneth didn't take up much of it.

"Would you like something to drink?" I asked.

"Something like what?" He still was not looking at me.

"Like a Sprite? Or a glass of milk?"

He shrugged. "I guess. A Sprite would be fine."

I got him a Sprite. He did not open it. He fidgeted a while longer and then said, "I guess you saw that math book I left in the plane."

"Yes, I did."

"I guess you think I did it. Killed them. My dad and Aunt Sue and that nice old cop."

"I'm not far enough into the investigation to know who did it. Any of it. And I have no idea whether you'd have a reason to kill Captain Millner or your Aunt Sue."

"I didn't have any reason. And I didn't say you knew. You can't know I did it because I didn't. I asked what you thought."

"And I answered," I said. "But I'll clarify what I said. No, I don't think you did it. But I haven't ruled you out. I also haven't ruled out your mother and several other people."

"You know who I think did it?"

"Who?" I asked. "And more to the point, why do you suspect whoever it is you suspect?"

I had to wait a while longer. Then he said, "Aren't you supposed to tell me that thing about you have a right to remain silent?"

"I already did that, a couple of days ago," I reminded him. "But if you like, I'll be glad to do it again. Since you came here, I assume you do want to talk with me, especially since you already told me that was what you wanted. But if you've changed your mind, the door isn't locked. If you want a ride home I'll take you. You have a right to remain silent—"

"You don't have to tell me that. I know it. I just was asking if you were supposed to. When I'm ready to go home I'll walk. That's the trouble with too many people nowadays. They think they don't have feet." He wiggled a little more, opened his Sprite, drank a couple of swallows, and then said, "The coach always says that. The one at that school in Maryland. I don't like him and he doesn't like me, but he's right about that. I came home because I was going crazy at school, but now I'm going crazy at home. There's four cops there all the time. *Four.* And my mom keeps crying and crying and crying and saying it's all her fault. So I asked her how was it her fault and she wouldn't tell me. And that stupid Dalmatian keeps sitting outside my dad's bedroom and howling. And he tried to bite one of the cops and he tried to bite Uncle Ken and he runs away whenever I try to pet him. Your dogs are nicer." He scratched Ivory's ears, and Ivory's stump of a tail swung in circles of joy. It was quite clear that in his mind, his pack had just been enlarged again. "This is a nice dog. And so is that caramel-colored one outside. What are their names?"

I told him, rather absently. I would be inclined to agree that Ivory was nicer, though probably stupider, than Polka. But I was really puzzled as to how Kenneth had managed to get on such good terms with Pat so fast. A pit bull is normally a very friendly dog to anyone who has been properly introduced to him, but those proper introductions are essential.

"Why can't Pat come inside?" he asked.

"He's just so rambunctious," I said. "But we've decided to start letting him in. Harry's going to get him a dog door."

"Any dog door he could get through, I could get through."

"That's one of the reasons we haven't gotten him a dog door yet," I pointed out. "A lot of burglars are your size or smaller. But Harry said with Pat, we wouldn't have to worry about burglars. Pat doesn't like very many people he doesn't know."

"I'm not a burglar," Kenneth said, "and Pat likes me even if he doesn't know me. But I'll bet he'd try to bite Uncle Ken too, just like Polka did."

"Maybe so. Who's your Uncle Ken?" I asked, though I thought I knew.

"Oh, you know, Aunt Sue's husband. They named me for him. I don't know why. He doesn't like me any more than my dad did. He came over to the house to look in the safe this morning, but it was empty because you guys—well, not you especially, but some cops—they took the money down to the police station, and there wasn't anything else in the safe. Uncle Ken says there was supposed to be some other stuff, and he's really mad. He thinks the cops took it, but Mom gave him the copy of the search warrant, you know, the copy that she kept, with the list of stuff the cops took away on it, and whatever it is he's looking for wasn't on the list, but he says the cops took it anyway."

I sat up straight, thinking back. I had been searching on the same warrant everybody else was searching on, but did the little green notebook ever get on the list of things seized? No, it probably didn't, because I was keeping my own list and I wasn't through yet. Or at least I hadn't been through, until the second computer disappeared.

Technically I could go right on searching on that warrant, because police had remained at the scene ever since that warrant had been served . . . even if one of the police was at the scene dead for a good many hours.

I had sent Danny Shea to the office with instructions to make his report, but I hadn't followed up to see that he did. I had dictated my report onto a tape recorder for Millie to type, but had I specified that a copy of my list of things taken from the building ought to be turned over to Jeanne?

Probably not.

I had been a little distracted, what with the death of Captain Millner and all that followed it.

And anyway, the notebook hadn't been in the safe. At the time we found the safe open it contained only money, and the notebook was hidden in Curtis's desk.

"Has he said anything about what he's looking for? What it might look like?" I asked.

Kenneth shook his head. "He hasn't really said much of anything. Mainly he's just been yelling."

"Just yelling in general or yelling at anybody in particular?"

"Yelling at my mom, mainly," Kenneth said. He drank more of the Sprite and for the first time let his back touch the chair back. He was beginning to relax; apparently he'd decided I wasn't going to do anything horrible to him.

"Is he still over there?" I asked.

"I don't know. Probably. He was looking all over the place. Look, I don't want to go back there," he said quickly, apparently thinking I was about to stand up. "I mean, he's not going to do anything to Mom, not with four cops there."

That was probably true, and after all, I did have a direct order not to go over there today, even to visit Jeanne.

"Is it him you suspect?"

Kenneth glanced at me in some obvious surprise. "No, why should I? Do you?"

"I told you I haven't reached any conclusions yet. I'm still looking at everybody."

"No," he said, and resumed fidgeting. I went on waiting, and after a while he said, "I don't suspect him. It's somebody else. And I really don't know anyway."

"All right," I said.

"But—when Mom was crying in her room and she didn't think I heard her, I think she was talking to somebody on the phone, and she said, 'But I couldn't let him go to prison.' And she cried some more and said, 'I didn't think. I should have realized but I just didn't *think*.' And I thought—maybe— Did you know my dad was a criminal?"

"Yes, I did."

"He wanted me to be one too. Can you imagine?" Kenneth was starting to cry now. "My own father wanted me to be a criminal! I had to go to this super-duper fancy school I hate, and I had to do all my homework and make straight As and be the captain of the football team, which I couldn't do in ten million years, by the way, and get on the National Honor Society and all that stuff, and for what? So that I could grow up and be a criminal like my father! I mean—who would do that to their kid? What kind of a man was he?"

"Not a very nice one, obviously," I said softly, and scooted the Kleenex box over to the corner of the coffee table.

"Thanks," Kenneth said, grabbing a tissue and blowing his nose. He was sobbing by now, and I let him cry, and he was hugging a damp cocker spaniel who smelled just like a damp cocker spaniel. The cocker spaniel licked his face; when Cameron had asked about that, I'd told him that was the way dogs kiss people.

It was a pretty sure thing Kenneth was getting more comfort from Ivory than he ever had from his father.

After a while he stopped crying, and he said, "I don't know who did it. I really don't. I'm just—scared. Because if Mom really thought Dad was going to prison—I keep thinking—she loved him, I don't know why but she did, and I just keep thinking, I guess, would she have killed him to keep him from going to prison? And then killed Aunt Sue and that nice old cop so she wouldn't get caught? And I don't know. I wish I didn't think she might but I do all the same. Not that she did. Just that she might have."

"Do you know who she was talking to on the phone?"

"No," he said. "She didn't ever say a name."

"Was it somebody she called, or somebody who called her?"

"It was somebody she called. At least I guess it was. I never heard the phone ring, so it must have been somebody she called."

Quite suddenly something popped into my head, and I barely had time to think it before I asked it. "You said Polka tried to bite one of the cops and tried to bite your Uncle Ken. Did he try to bite Daniel Ellis?"

Kenneth stared at me. "Mr. Ellis didn't go to the house. Why did you think he did?"

"Well, since he brought you here, and since he and your dad worked together—"

"Yeah, but they were mad at each other," Kenneth said. "I mean, Mr. Ellis flew me here to Fort Worth because he was coming here anyway, but he said he didn't want to get even into the same *neighborhood* with my dad because he was afraid my dad would take it out on me. So I was just supposed to say I hitched home. I did have to walk about five miles or something like that. And it was dark. And cold."

I remembered the morning distinctly. It was indeed dark and cold. And Mr. Ellis let Kenneth out five miles away? That would be more than an hour's walk for most people; for Kenneth, small for his age and unwilling to run, it would be at least an hour and a half.

Wheels were beginning to turn inside my head.

Quite suddenly, Kenneth burst into tears. Real tears now. The mock arrogance I had seen in him was gone, and only with its leaving did I realize how phony, how put on it was. "I don't want to go home," he sobbed, "and I don't want to go back to that school. Can I stay here? Just for a while?"

Automatically I looked around for Harry. I couldn't possibly make such a decision by myself.

Harry had heard; he was up, standing in the doorway and

rather leaning on the right side of it. "Same like Lori?" I asked quickly, hoping he'd understand what I meant.

He nodded. "Sounds great."

I turned back to Kenneth. "You'd have to share a room with our five-year-old," I said, "and we do have rules. If you stayed here we'd treat you like a member of the family, and that means following our rules and doing chores. And if your mother agrees you don't have to go back to school in Maryland, you would have to transfer and go to school here. I couldn't possibly have you here and not in school."

"At a public school?" he asked, his voice sounding rather suspicious.

"Certainly at a public school." Maybe he wouldn't want to go to a public school.

"And I'd ride a school bus?"

"Usually." Maybe he wouldn't want to ride a school bus.

And maybe I'd like him better if he hadn't spent several days making himself as unlikable as possible.

"That would be great," he said.

"You realize I have to let your mother know where you are and be sure it's okay with her," I said, with a sinking feeling that I already knew that Jeanne would say yes and Harry and I would say yes, which effectively we had already done, and I hadn't the slightest idea how long "just a while" would turn out to be, and I really wasn't overwhelmingly fond of this kid.

But I knew me just as well as Harry did. I couldn't even turn away a somewhat chewed-up stray pit bull, a stray long-haired cat that had not been groomed since her birth two years earlier, or a cocker spaniel whose owner had just burglarized my house. How in the world was I going to turn away a twelve-year-old boy, especially one whose world—such as it was, which wasn't great—had just blown up in his face?

Obviously I was not going to. Obviously Harry was not going to.

I didn't have to look up Jeanne's number. I had called it often enough in the last few days.

# 3

GARY SAID I COULDN'T GO TO VISIT JEANNE. He didn't say Jeanne couldn't come to visit me.

She showed up with two of her police escorts; the other two presumably were still at the house, in case Captain Millner's killer came back one more time to do something else he hadn't done in the earlier trips.

She had some of Kenneth's summer clothes with her. "I'm sorry," she said, "but all his winter stuff is in Maryland. You said you have a son; could Kenneth borrow something of his?"

"My son," I said, "is six foot five. And he's in Nevada."

"Oh dear," she said inadequately. "Well, I'll just have to go out and get him something."

"Mom," Kenneth said distinctly, "I don't want you to pick out my clothes. I can pick out my own clothes."

"But—"

"I can pick out my own clothes. I've still got that Visa card you gave me. I've never used it, but I've got it. I guess I can go get clothes with it."

"Well, I guess you can," Jeanne said doubtfully, looking at me. "But I don't think Deb likes to go shopping on Sunday."

Kenneth looked at me. "Why not?"

"Because it's the Sabbath."

"What's the Sabbath?"

I could see that I was going to have a few problems with this boy. I remembered the "house rules" I had posted in Hal's bedroom when some of his friends got a little rowdy one time and we wound up having to repaint Hal's room entirely—twice—to get rid of the graffiti, which had been drawn on the walls with a black permanent marker. It was time to get those out again. And there was something good about Harry's computer fetish: the rules were stored. And so, come to think of it, was the form we'd used when Lori first came to live with us, before we became her legal guardians.

"Let me go do some stuff on the computer," I said. "I'll be right back."

Harry did not offer to go attend to the computer, about which he is far more knowledgeable than I am. Instead, he sat down in the living room to get acquainted with Jeanne and Kenneth.

If I remembered correctly, Harry had downloaded all of his files from his old computer into his new one, and it shouldn't be too hard to find.

It wasn't.

### RALSTON HOUSE RULES

In this house you may:

Talk.
Read.
Play board games if you put all the pieces away properly when you're through.
Play computer games if nobody else is using the computer and the games aren't violent or otherwise objectionable.
Tell jokes.
Laugh.
Gather around the drums and keyboard in the garage and play and sing.
Go in the kitchen and make snacks (as long as you clean up after yourselves).
Watch television, as long as the shows are decent.
Watch videos, as long as they're fit to be seen in a

Christian household.

Dance on the back deck, provided you don't turn the music so high it bothers the neighbors.

Write graffiti on the whiteboard (as long as it is not vulgar, does not refer to bodily functions, and does not disturb what is already there, like appointments and grocery lists).

YOU MAY NOT:

Drink.

Smoke. (If you feel you MUST smoke you must go to the park to do it. Hal's mother is very allergic to tobacco smoke.)

Do drugs.

Swear.

Write on the walls.

Write obnoxious graffiti on the whiteboard.

Fornicate.

ALL OF HAL'S GUESTS ARE BOUND BY THESE RULES. SO ARE ALL OTHER GUESTS.

Although he grumbled a little, Hal actually was rather proud of those rules; pointing them out to his friends took at least part of the onus of keeping his friends under control off of him. He kept them posted on the wall of his room long after the necessity passed, and when he left to go on his mission he carefully put the rules away with his books.

"These are the rules," I told Kenneth briskly. "If you can't abide by them, then you don't want to stay here."

He read them, with Jeanne looking over his shoulder. He looked at Jeanne and said, "Mom, can I stay here?"

She patted him on the hand. "I think that would be a very good idea. At least for now, till things—settle down. We don't have to make any long-range decisions yet."

"But can I start going to public school?"

"That you certainly can do," she said. "I'm not going to send you back to Maryland, and our house and Deb's house are in the same school district."

I walked outside with Jeanne. There was no delicate way to ask this question, so I took the plunge: "Do you know what he's worried about?"

"Who wouldn't be worried, with all this stuff going on?" Jeanne said. She was wrapped snugly in a new-looking parka, and she looked like someone who would be in a television commercial advertising skiing or skiwear.

"Jeanne, he's worried because he heard your end of a telephone conversation." I related the conversation.

Jeanne stood quite still for a moment. Then she said, "He was quite mistaken. He didn't hear any such thing."

"Jeanne—"

"I told you he was mistaken! Thank you for taking care of him, but he didn't hear anything like that!" She ran to her car, slammed the door, and peeled out as she drove away.

# 4

**D**EB?" HARRY ASKED. "ARE YOU AWAKE?"

"Oh, sure, I'm always awake at—" I squinted at the clock— "two A.M. Why?"

"I'm sorry I woke you. I was just thinking."

"About what?"

"About—" He rolled over, stared at the ceiling. "About Captain Millner. I think I was jealous of Captain Millner."

"Why?" Suddenly I was somewhat more awake.

"I didn't think he'd do anything wrong. And I didn't think you would. It was just—you and he had such a good relationship. And sometimes it seemed like he was seeing more of you than I was. I didn't know I was jealous. Not until after he died, and I started thinking and trying to sort out how I felt, and— He was a terrific human being. I should have made an effort to get to know him better. Who's taking over his job?"

"Gary Hollister," I said. "And they want me to take over Gary's."

"What did you tell them?"

"I told them I didn't want to. But then Gary told me Captain Millner and he had already discussed it with each other and with the chief. But—I don't know, Harry, why would I want to be a lieutenant?"

"Why wouldn't you want to be a lieutenant?"

I'd have to think about that one.

This time, Harry went to sleep before I did.

And just before I dozed off, I thought drowsily, *The FBI has a tap on the Minot phone. I can find out what that conversation was about.*

# IX

MONDAY, NOVEMBER 15

# 1

---

**D**UB CALLED ME BEFORE I WAS EVEN OUT of bed on Monday. "You've got to work with me today," he said without preamble. "I checked with Gary and he said it's okay."

"I was planning on it," I replied sleepily, "and Gary okayed it Saturday. But what's so urgent that you needed to call at—" I looked at the clock and changed my wording— "before six o'-clock?"

"Is it that early?" He sounded amazed.

"Yes, Dub, it's that early."

"Sorry—I got up at four-thirty so I could get as much done as possible before the phones started ringing. I've been so busy this morning I haven't looked at my watch, and it feels like about seven." (*It might feel that way to me,* I thought, *if I had gotten up at four-thirty,* which is something I never under any imaginable circumstances feel like doing.) "Anyway, I need you because first thing this morning I want to talk with Nudara Bint Akram Umm Jamil Akhbar—that name is quite a mouthful—and when I tried to talk with her Saturday she told me, in Arabic, through her son who translated what she said, that she won't talk with me. She says she will talk only to a woman, and she won't talk to anybody from the FBI."

From some of my voracious reading—all right, I'll admit it, from a couple of Tarzan novels and two or three Harlequin romances—I remembered a few Arabic prepositions, and I said, "The name just means she's Nudara the daughter of Akram and the mother of Jamil, and her family name is Akhbar. I don't know whether she'd use the family name in her own country or not. But if you know what it means it doesn't sound like such a mouthful. How do you know she'll talk to me?"

"This is her country now; they're all naturalized citizens," Dub said. "You mean country of origin. And I don't know for sure that she'll talk to you, but you're a woman and you're not in the FBI."

"Does she not speak English?"

"I haven't the slightest idea. I think she probably does, though, because she's running the gasoline station by herself a good bit of the time, and she'd have to know at least some English to know what her customers want."

"Gasoline station?" I repeated, and then remembered that her husband, now in prison, had owned a service station. I don't know why I had assumed it would have been lost or sold; I shouldn't have been surprised that she was keeping it going. Resignedly I asked, "Okay, Dub, do you want me to meet you somewhere, or do you want to pick me up at home? I've got to get dressed and eat something. And listen—"

"I'll pick you up," he interrupted.

"Dub—" I tried to say.

Too late. He had already hung up.

I did the *69 bit to get the number he was calling from. A recorded voice informed me that that was a private number which could not be released, but if I wished to call it I could press "1" on my phone. I did, only to be told that number could not be reached at the moment. The telephone would go on trying, and call me back with a distinctive ring when the call was going through.

It took about five minutes for the "distinctive ringing" to finally ring.

"Dub," I said when he answered, "I need you to get some information."

"Okay, what?"

"The tap on the Minots' telephone line. There was a conversation yesterday that I need to hear."

"The tap was dropped as soon as we heard Minot was dead," Dub answered. "The court order covered only him, so we couldn't keep it on. What was the conversation?"

I told him, wishing I hadn't quit swearing when I did. There are times when "Oh, rats!" is just not expressive enough.

"That sounds interesting," Dub said.

"Yeah, it did to me too. That's why I hoped you still had the tap going."

"Sorry. I'll pick you up about nine. I think I'm going to get some more information beforehand. I've got something working that came up all of a sudden, right after I got through calling you just a minute ago."

Nine! Oh joy, oh bliss! I did not have to hurry, not even as much as I did on a normal morning when I had to leave the house by seven to be at muster by eight. And nobody official would care that I'd spent the extra time at home. I had accumulated another ten hours of comp time on Saturday, on top of the hundreds of hours I already had stacked up, and theoretically I could take off just about any time I wanted to. Theoretically is not actually. Actually, about 90 percent of the time in the past when I wanted time off, Captain Millner would tell me that of course I had the right to take my comp time, but this just wasn't a good time to do it.

What would happen with Gary and comp time? Theoretically I had been working under Gary for many years; actually, my interaction with him had been fairly limited, because I usually wound up on cases Captain Millner was greatly interested in.

Anyway, this day I had some time of my own, and I was pleased.

I made breakfast—fast but unimaginative scrambled eggs and toast—saw Harry and Lori off, issued Kenneth a door key, and then bundled Cameron and Kenneth into the car. I dropped Cameron by the day-care center, which would see to getting him to and from kindergarten, and then, armed with the form Jeanne had signed, got Kenneth registered in school.

It took longer to find out how much money the student fees entailed than it did to fill out paperwork. But I wrote the appropriate checks, filled out the appropriate paperwork, made sure Kenneth had lunch money and knew what school bus to get on in the afternoon, and still managed to get home before Dub arrived.

# 2

I WAS NOT USED TO SEEING GASOLINE pumped and tires and fluid levels checked by a woman wearing a voluminous black chador, blue jeans, socks, and sneakers.

We did some preliminary verbal fencing during which I identified myself; someone else—a tall, dark young man I thought might be her son, Jamil—took over the gas pump; and we—Nudara and I—sat down inside the service station, on a couch made of what looked like an old station wagon rear seat. Somewhere during the preliminaries we had agreed that she was to call me Deb and I was to call her Nudara.

It did not matter what Dub called her, because she refused to respond to anything he said. She did, however, agree that he could listen to the conversation she and I were having, as long as he was willing to stand and listen. The seating was for us two women only.

Dub was then nudged over a bit as the dark young man came in, closed and locked the door and put a "closed" sign on it, and scootched around the counter to turn the keys to cut off the pumps. This left Dub standing perilously near a tall stack of tires, with the dark young man sitting on a high stool in front of the cash register. The office was about as claustrophobic as my kitchen.

I will not say that Nudara's English was perfect. I will say that it was fully understandable.

There were several other things that I realized very quickly:

First, she believed her husband was innocent of the crimes for which he was imprisoned. So, by now, did I.

Second, she was a very angry woman. I considered her anger fully understandable and justified.

And third, she was far more knowledgeable about her scriptures than I was about mine, a fact which I found profoundly embarrassing even though she had had the same religion all her life and I'd had mine only a little over a year. (Harry had permitted Hal to become a Mormon when he wanted to, but Vicky, of course, was out of the nest by then and Becky was headed that way before I started attending regularly. I had been going to church for over four years before deciding to be baptized.)

Dub started about four times to speak to Nudara. Each time, she put her hands over her ears. Not only was she not willing to speak to him, she was not even willing to let him speak to her.

Finally he said, "Deb, will you please tell Mrs. Akhbar that if she is willing to cooperate with us on this, there's a very good chance that we can prove that her husband didn't commit any crime."

She shot a quick glance at him then before drawing the filmy black fabric—dyed muslin, I thought, but wasn't sure—more closely around her face.

"And of course, if we prove that, then we can get him out of prison," Dub said, "and probably get him some kind of recompense for the miscarriage of justice in this case."

Dutifully I conveyed the message, although all four of us knew it had already been understood.

Even then Nudara wasn't quite willing to begin discussing facts. She wanted to discuss scripture first. To be more precise, she intended to quote or paraphrase a goodly chunk of her own scriptures, and she intended to preach a sermon.

She adjusted her veiling again and then said, "I must explain to you my husband." She paused to be sure we were listening. Then she said, "Allah has said through his prophet:

'Unto each nation have we given sacred rites which they are to perform; so let them not dispute with thee of the matter.' My family came from Palestine, and our sacred rites are those of Islam, which means obedience to Allah. Most people in your country think all followers of Islam are terrorists. That is not true."

I waited to be sure she was through speaking for a moment, as I didn't want to interrupt her; then I said, "My scriptures say that 'the Lord doth grant unto all nations, of their own nation and tongue, to teach his word, yea, in wisdom, all that he seeth fit that they should have.' Our nation also has been given prophets. And I know that only a few out of any people are evil." (In fact, Harry and I both had often warned our children that generalizations about people tend to be offenses against humanity as well as against common sense. We had started out with the intention of raising no racist children, and in that we had succeeded.)

Clearly I had surprised Nudara, and for the first time I felt she was really looking at me. I had become a person rather than a part of a machine that had done its best to crush her family.

"Allah has said: 'Whoso cometh guilty unto his Lord, verily for him is hell.' " She glanced at me out of the corner of one eye, and I felt I was in the biggest wrestling match of my entire life.

I thought fast and hard, and then said, "The Bible says: 'The wicked shall be turned into hell, and all the nations that forget God.' "

She said, "We are People of the Book, you and I."

"We try to be," I agreed.

"Then you will understand. The prophet Muhammad has said: 'Hold fast, all of you together, to the cable of Allah.' "

That one was easy. I said, "The prophet Nephi has said: 'the rod of iron . . . [is] the word of God, which [leads] to the fountain of living waters.' "

This time she actually smiled before saying, "Allah has said: 'There is no compulsion in religion.' " She looked at me challengingly.

That one took me a minute. Then I said, "God has said: 'in the Garden of Eden, gave I unto man his agency.'"

She sat up straighter and said, "My husband believes these things. I believe these things. My son believes these things." She glanced at the tall young man, and then continued, "Allah has said: 'Whoever has done evil and his sin surrounds him; such are rightful owners of the Fire; they will abide therein.'"

When I started to speak, she held up her hand to stop me. She was through playing scripture chase; she said, "Allah has said: 'He who takes Satan for a comrade, a bad comrade hath he,' Allah has said: 'Those whom the angels take in death, the angels will ask: "What were you doing?" If they say, "We did evil because we were oppressed in the land," the angels will say: "Was not Allah's earth spacious that ye could have migrated therein?" For such people, their habitation will be hell, an evil journey's end.'" She took a deep breath. "My husband truly believes these things and shows his belief by his actions. Our grandparents owned a rich orange grove, in a plot of land our forebears had farmed for a thousand years. When Israel was recreated, Israel seized the orange groves and the houses wherein our people dwelt, and drove us out, and tore down the houses and cut down the orange trees, and built a kibbutz on the land of our inheritance. Then we had no land. We lived in the desert, in tents. There was no water; we had to bring water from other people's wells to drink, and we washed our hands with sand. Among our people, some fought to get their land back, and as we grew up we saw the rich earth flow with blood. I married my cross-cousin, as is proper among my people: my husband is my mother's brother's son. After we were married, my husband said to me, 'Israel will never return to us the land of our inheritance, but Allah's earth is spacious. We will migrate therein, rather than fill the earth with strife.' We came to this country, and our son was born here. We were not blessed with more children." (Having given birth to only one of my four children, the youngest, after adopting the first three, I could sympathize with her on that score.) "We worked, and we became citizens of this country. My husband bought this gasoline station and we have worked at it. Yet *that man"*—she gestured toward Dub—"is one of those who took my husband to prison, claiming that for two truckloads of gasoline Ashraf, a man who would not shed blood even to regain the lands of his inheritance, would commit murder. My son has a college degree in criminal justice, and he cannot find work of his choosing, because the police departments think all Muslims are murderers. Certainly there are fools and murderers who claim to follow Islam. Are there no fools and murderers who claim to be Christian or Jewish? Yet the Muslims and the Christians and the Jews are all of the People of the Book, the ones to whom the Law has been given. No others on the face of the earth have been given the Law."

Her voice was shaking with rage, and for a moment I had no words to say. I finally replied, "I'm sure there are more fools and murderers in any religion, in any nation, than any of us would like to think about; but there are more good people than bad in any religion, in any nation. And I believe you are telling me the truth. I believe that your husband was greatly wronged, and that your son is being wronged, and that you are the most wronged of all. Nudara, please help us. If you help us I believe that we can learn and prove the truth. And—once when the Prophet Joseph Smith was imprisoned unjustly, he called to God for help, and God said—I don't remember the exact words, but it's something like this: 'If you are dragged to prison and your enemies prowl around you like wolves; and if you are thrown into a pit, or into the hands of murderers, and the sentence of death is passed upon you; if you are cast into the ocean and the waves conspire against you; if fierce winds become your enemy, or the skies darken and all the elements combine to get in your way; and even if the very jaws of hell shall open to swallow you; be aware that all these things shall give you experience, and ultimately be for your good.' I don't know why these awful things happened to your family, but if your husband is the kind of man you've told me he is—and I believe what you have said—he'll come out of prison even stronger than he was when he went in."

Nudara took a deep breath and looked rather than glanced at Dub. "Are you trying now to get my husband out of prison, after you helped to put him in?"

Dub said, "I didn't want to arrest your husband to start with. I believed him then, but there was too much evidence against him, and the federal prosecutor insisted we take the warrant. I told the judge, both before and after the conviction, that I wasn't convinced he was guilty, and I personally asked the judge to put him on probation and I was angry when he refused. I still don't think your husband is guilty, and if there's a way to do it, yes, I want to get him out of prison."

Nudara looked at the tall young man. "Shall we trust them, Jamil?" she asked.

"Yes," Jamil said.

Dub took a deep breath. "Is it all right now for me to speak?"

"You may speak," Jamil said, in perfectly colloquial, unaccented English, "but you may not sit with my mother."

Dub started asking questions, essentially walking them through the entire situation again—hijacking, murder, gasoline sales, tank truck parked behind the service station—just as they had already told it time and time again.

They didn't actually have much new information for us. This hijacking and murder had occurred after Curtis's accident, so the actual hijacker, the actual killer, couldn't possibly have been Curtis; not that we had ever thought he was. The Curtis Minots of this world always make sure their hands look clean.

As far as anybody could remember, Ashraf had been alone in the gasoline station when the man who identified himself as Curtis Minot had called him. Some years back Ashraf had bought gasoline from Minot several times before, and he hadn't met Minot face to face over any of those deals either. All of those times the delivery had been ordinary: Ashraf had paid the oil company as he normally paid oil companies. That made sense; we knew Curtis had a lot of legitimate business to camouflage most of his illegitimate business.

Jamil, but not Nudara, had been at the station with Ashraf when the first of the two hijacked deliveries was made; Nudara, but not Jamil, had been there when the second delivery was made. All three had agreed on the description of the driver, and although Nudara and Jamil had each seen the driver only once, there was no reason why they should doubt Ashraf's statement that it was the same man both times.

The description of the man fit the description of the man the surviving driver saw flagging him down.

Unfortunately, the description also fit Ashraf.

The Identikit portrait that was produced, based on the word of all three of the Akhbars and of the driver, actually looked quite a lot like Saddam Hussein, though we were all pretty certain he wasn't.

All of this, Dub pointed out, was in the case file. None of it was new.

I didn't know why we expected to get anything new. Obviously we needed it, but that didn't mean it was there to get.

Jamil and Nudara agreed that the man was not in fact Arabic or Palestinian, and was not a Muslim at all. "He ate his lunch in our station, while the gasoline was going into the tank in the ground," Nudara said, "and he was eating swineflesh."

"Pork?" I asked rather fuzzily.

"A ham sandwich," Nudara clarified. "We do not eat swineflesh."

"I didn't know that," I said.

"*Al-Qur'ân* forbids the eating of swineflesh," Nudara said. Then she gave us the first, very small, new bit of real information, as she added, "My husband asked him to take his sandwich wrapper away. We did not want to touch it, and we did not want it in the wastebasket of our place of business. It is an abomination. He and my husband were sitting on this couch, and I was at the cash register except when I was outside pumping gas. When the men were through eating, I was going to eat, and my husband would pump the gas and attend the cash register. The man stood up to take his sandwich wrapper away, and he took my husband's sandwich wrapper also. Then he went around the side of the building, and I supposed he was going to the men's room. I thought he was going to put the wrappers in the toilet and flush it, and Ashraf went after him to tell him not to do that, because the wrappers were heavy plastic and might stop up the toilet. He said he would not. That I know he said. I heard it."

"Did you see the wrappers again?" Dub asked.

"No. But I was sitting on the couch eating and reading when the man left in his truck."

"What did your husband have in his sandwich bag?" I asked.

"Chicken. A chicken sandwich with lettuce and tomato and cucumbers and mayonnaise."

"Maybe we can get any crumbs left in the bag analyzed," Dub said. "Or it might have already been done. Can either of you think of anything, anything at all, that we might not have taken into consideration?"

"He did not speak Arabic," Nudara said. "He spoke English to us, but his English sounded odd."

"Odd how?" I asked.

"He sounded Hispanic," Jamil said abruptly. "Not Tex-Mex, not Spanglish. He sounded like a real Hispanic. Lower Central America or, more likely, South America. Not Spain, though. I'm sure of that."

"Why didn't you tell me this at the time?" Dub asked.

"I told another person from the FBI," Jamil said. "I assumed he had told you."

"If he did I don't remember it," Dub said, "and I think I would. I want to go and get something for both of you to look at. It'll probably take me an hour, hour and a half, to find it and get back here. Will you both still be here?"

# 3

---

**W**HERE DID YOU GET ALL THAT STUFF YOU were telling her?" Dub asked in the car. "Did you make it up? I've certainly never seen all of that in my Bible, at least so far as I know." He paused, looking thoughtful, and then added, "Of course, I never have read the whole Bible."

"I have more scriptures than just the Bible," I answered, "and I have read them all. It's all there, trust me. Okay, let's try to figure out what we've got so far."

What we had so far was interesting but I couldn't decide yet whether any of it was useful; we were now on our way to Dub's office to look at the original case folder and see what did and didn't jibe. And clearly Dub had something on his mind that he was not yet ready to tell me.

What he did tell me on the way in was that he had spent the entire weekend, except when he was catching an hour or two of sleep now and then on a couch in his office, running records checks on every person listed in that little green book, and calling FBI agents all over the country to do some overtime work, going to check on possible grudges and possible alibis, even if it was the weekend, even if it was wet, even if it was dark, even if it was snowing a few places in the country.

He'd been able to rule out a good many people that way, including some of the people on our hot list. Dan Sutherland, whose father's oil had been stolen, was out of the country, working with a joint U.S. and Russian oil exploration team in Siberia. (I had a hunch that I wouldn't like Siberia in mid-November, so I was glad it was him and not me.) Santiago Ramirez was definitely ruled out; we'd found out that he had been fatally knifed by another inmate in the federal prison in Atlanta several months ago.

We'd already agreed, Dub and I, that Bran Caley was out. We agreed now that all the Akhbars were clear.

That didn't leave us very many people to look at.

We could look at Jeanne again. We could look at Kenneth again. We could look at Ken Rimer, whom we hadn't really looked at very hard yet.

And we could look at Daniel Ellis, always assuming, of course, that we could *find* Daniel Ellis.

But Dub wanted to do something else first, and, maddeningly, he wouldn't tell me what. He just told me to wait and see.

The case file on the gasoline hijackings was on his desk, and he started sorting through papers. "Ah, there it is!" he said triumphantly, and pulled out a laboratory analysis sheet.

Inside the sandwich wrapper, along with the pistol, were bread crumbs, a trace of mayonnaise, a trace of chicken, several tomato seeds with the pulp still surrounding them, a shred of lettuce, and a bit of cucumber skin.

Nudara's memory had been accurate. And the explanation of Ashraf's fingerprints inside the sandwich bag was obviously correct . . . why hadn't anybody in the prosecutor's office considered the significance of the fact that none of Ashraf's fingerprints were *inside* the truck cab, or that the outside of the sandwich bag had deliberately been wiped clean?

Because it had been. On that kind of surface, from a hand with a little oily residue on it, immersion in water doesn't do away with fingerprints. All the ident tech has to do is let the plastic bag air dry and then very carefully process the surface of the plastic; most often SuperGlue fuming is used, though a good fine grade of magnetic fingerprint powder might also be used.

It was perfectly impossible for a used sandwich bag to

have no prints at all on it, though it was perfectly possible and indeed likely that the bag would have no *good* prints on it.

But all this bag had on the outside was smear marks.

While I was reading the lab report, Dub was on the telephone; he got off it and went over to watch his fax machine intently for about five minutes, while nothing happened on it. "Well, it'll take it a while to get done," he muttered, half to himself. "Let's talk about Daniel Ellis."

"What about Daniel Ellis?" I asked.

"He doesn't have any kind of record. He was never in the military. He has no fingerprints or photograph on file in any law enforcement agency that exchanges data with the FBI. He has a big house in Baltimore, Maryland, the kind you and I would call a mansion. And he insists that all his income is derived from servicing vending machines."

"You've got to be kidding."

"I am not kidding."

"Is that what the IRS says?" I asked.

"The IRS is not allowed to give us information unless we subpoena it," Dub said, "and I haven't had time. That's what my contacts in Maryland say. They'd been trying to get a court order to get a tap on Ellis's phone, but the judge said there wasn't enough probable cause yet."

*Probable cause* is a legal term that causes law enforcement agencies a lot of pain and misery, though I could understand both its historical importance and its present value. It is not, and should not be, legal for any law enforcement agency to tap anybody's phone anytime it wants to. The checks and balances are essential to keep the system honest.

The fax came through, or at least *a* fax came through, and Dub dashed joyously over to get it. Yes, it was the one he'd been waiting for. "Look," he said, and pulled out a mug shot from the case folder and put it beside the fax.

I looked.

The fax consisted of five near-photo-quality mug shots, all on one sheet of paper. All of them were of men in their mid-forties, men who, to judge by their faces, could have been of Middle Eastern origin or could have been of mixed Spanish and Native American origin.

The single mug shot from the case folder was not the same mug shot as the one on the upper left corner of the fax, but it was perfectly obvious that it was the same person, unless the two were identical twins.

"Who?" I asked.

"Santiago Ramirez," Dub said.

"But he's dead," I pointed out.

"I know," Dub said. "So now let's go back out to the Akhbars' service station."

# 4

DUB WANTED THE TWO OF US TO SPEAK privately first with Jamil and then with Nudara.

Jamil vetoed that. Dub could speak privately with Jamil, but the only one who was going to speak privately with Nudara was me. "It is not appropriate," Jamil said, "for a woman to speak alone with a man."

It didn't really matter, though. Nudara picked out the picture of Ramirez instantly. So did Jamil.

"Will you now go and arrest this evil person," Nudara said, "and make him admit that my husband is innocent?"

"I wish we could," Dub said, "but he's dead. Don't worry, though, we're not through."

"But Dub," I said, "you told me that all through Ramirez's trial he kept trying to prove that Minot was more guilty than he was, but all he ever talked about was drug smuggling. Why wouldn't he have mentioned this?"

"He didn't dare," Dub said softly. "Think about it."

I thought about it.

"Of course," I said. "He couldn't, because to do so he'd have to admit he'd killed a man."

"Exactly," Dub said. "To the best of our knowledge—and this is based not just on suspicion but also on evidence such that we knew he was guilty but we didn't have enough to take to court—this was the only time that anybody was killed in any of Minot's or Ellis's operations or any of their joint operations. Minot clearly did *not* want anybody killed. Ramirez exceeded his instructions. And that was why Minot ratted on him, and why the Border Patrol caught him on his next border crossing. As long as Ramirez kept his mouth shut, all anybody could get him for was smuggling; he'd wind up in the federal prison in Atlanta as in fact he did, and with luck he'd have been out in five years or so, no matter how long his sentence officially was. He had no way of knowing he'd be murdered in prison, so he expected to get home eventually. But if he had confessed to murder in the course of robbery, he'd have gone to the Texas prison in Huntsville, and quite probably he'd have landed on Death Row."

"So he let my innocent husband go to prison in his place," Nudara said bitterly.

"We'll get your husband out," Dub said. "And—I've never read the Koran. But from what I heard you quoting today, doesn't it have a good bit to say about eternal punishment for the guilty?"

Nudara began, slowly, to smile. "*Al-Qur'ân* says much about that. Evildoers will not escape the wrath of Allah."

"I don't know how long it will take," Dub said. "If I can reach the right people fast enough, we might have him out in a couple of weeks, but it could be as long as a couple of months. Can you live with that?"

"I suppose we have no choice," Jamil said.

Dub tucked the fax back into his briefcase. "What kind of police work are you interested in?"

"Any kind," Jamil said.

"Once this is all wrapped up, why don't you give me a call?" Dub handed over his business card.

Jamil looked at it, showed it to his mother, and put it into his billfold.

# 5

THIS TIME WE HAD A SEARCH WARRANT.

The federal judge had agreed that with everything that was going on, and the known close connection between Curtis Minot and Daniel Ellis, we had a right to see what was in Ellis's apartment in Fort Worth. He'd also agreed to notify one of his colleagues in Maryland, who would issue to FBI agents there a search warrant for Ellis's house.

A search warrant comes in two parts. The first part is the affidavit; in it the officer states, under oath, what he expects to find in the area to be searched, and why he expects to find it. What is his probable cause? What is his source of information? (It's legal to refuse to name an informant, but in that case the officer must state that this is an informant who has been used before in at least three cases, which of course means that in the first three cases the informant's information must be backed up by information from at least one other source, one already verified.) Two copies of the affidavit are printed, and the court keeps one. The other goes into the investigators' case folder.

Three copies of the search warrant—which gives permission to search when signed by the judge—are printed. All three are kept at the location to be searched while the searching is going on, and a description of everything seized under the warrant is written on an addendum to each copy of the warrant. One copy is then left with the person who controls the premises that were searched, or, if no one is present except law enforcement officers, it is left on display in a prominent place in the premises that were searched. One copy is returned to the judge who issued the warrant, to be filed with the affidavit, and the third copy goes into the officers' case folder.

Showing the warrant to the desk clerk was enough to get us the keys to Ellis's apartment, though the desk clerk insisted upon accompanying us to make sure we did no damage.

We might as well not have bothered to get the keys; the desk clerk might as well have stayed at his post.

The door wasn't locked, and the damage was already done.

# 6

AFTER A FEW MOMENTS OF INCOHERENCE, the desk clerk confirmed that the body was that of the man he'd known as Daniel Ellis.

This was a state crime, not a federal crime, and Dub handed me his cellular phone so that I could call my office.

Curtis Minot had been shot once in the head. Sue Rimer and Scott Millner had both been poisoned.

Like Minot, Daniel Ellis had been shot.

Unlike Minot, Daniel Ellis had been shot twelve times; the weapon, as I could tell from the empty brass scattered around the room, was some kind of 9 mm automatic or semiautomatic, and whoever did it probably had stopped at least once to reload.

The other three seemed to have been thoroughly thought out, passionless, removal of road blocks.

This was a murder of blind rage.

I thought I knew who'd done it, and I thought I knew why; even if I hadn't already figured it out, the presence on the living room floor of two computers and a stack of diskettes would have given me a pretty good idea. How was another matter; in fact, that question had me totally baffled.

Of course I couldn't leave yet, even to search for the killer. I had to stay while Andrew Habib from the medical examiner's office came and pronounced Daniel Ellis dead, and told me he'd been dead probably about sixteen hours, give or take two or three hours either way. That would take it back into sometime Sunday night. Then I had to wait for Bob Castle and Sarah Collins to arrive to begin the crime scene work, so that I could tell them what I particularly wanted them to look for.

The federal search warrant was in Dub's name, not mine. He had to stay there while the entire premises were searched, but I didn't.

The fact that I had arrived in Dub's car could have posed a problem, except that by the time I called my office I had already decided what to do about it. I asked Bob and Sarah to come in separate cars and then turn one of the cars over to me, and to bring me a hand radio.

I told Dub where I was going, and I left.

MONDAY, NOVEMBER 15

# 1

In the past Captain Millner had said quite a lot about what he considered my bad habit of going to talk with suspects or serve search warrants by myself. This complaint had been repeated monotonously often by Gary Hollister, who was now my supervisor; and Harry has had even more to say about it than either of them.

The fact remained that I stood a chance of getting information if I went in by myself; if I took other people with me, I probably wouldn't get anything.

That was a judgment call. And if the police department wanted to make me a lieutenant, it had better understand from the start that my judgment calls, good or bad, were my own to make.

My first stop was Ken Rimer. The last I had heard, his wife's body had not yet been released by the medical examiner's office, so I hoped that he was at home waiting. I thought about telephoning him first, but I didn't want to risk spooking him. So I just drove to his house, told the dispatcher where I was and what I would be doing and suggested that if he couldn't reach me by radio at fifteen minute intervals he dispatch another car to my location, and went and knocked on the door.

Ken Rimer answered, attired somewhat like Harry on a particularly bad weekend. He was unshaven; his hair hadn't been combed; it was somewhat obvious that he hadn't bathed or brushed his teeth; he had on dirty khaki pants, a dirty

T-shirt, and dirty black nylon socks; and the alcohol on his breath was enough to fell an ox.

He recognized me, however, and stood back from the door to let me in.

"Ken," I said, "I'm here as cop, not as friend. Do I still get to come in?"

"You got a warrant?"

"No, would you rather I go and get one?"

He shook his head. "What difference does it make? Come on in."

Sue had been dead less than three full days, but already the living room had that neglected look a house gets so quickly. Nothing had been dusted, the carpet hadn't been vacuumed, and petals had fallen off a bunch of chrysanthemums in a brass bowl onto the brass tray below. The air in the room felt stale, all the curtains were closed, and the lamp Ken turned on did little to dispel the gloom.

"Sit down," Ken said. "Can I get you anything?"

I sat down on the sofa. "No thank you," I said. "All I want now is the truth. You have the right to remain silent—"

He stared at me as I finished the litany. Then he said, "Hand it over."

I did. He signed. We had no witnesses, but it didn't matter, because I had no intention whatever of making a case against Ken Rimer. What had happened to his life was punishment enough, as far as I was concerned. The DA's office might not agree, but if it didn't, my guess was that Rimer would plead guilty to whatever anybody wanted to charge him with.

"Don't even think about playing games with me, Ken," I said. "I know enough of it already, and there are people who know where I am right now. Just tell me the truth. Daniel Ellis killed Curtis, didn't he?"

Ken sat down in a chair near me. "Yes," he said in an almost inaudible tone.

"How'd he get in?"

Ken shook his head. "I don't know that."

"Who killed Sue?"

Ken started sobbing, and I waited. Finally he lifted his head to look at me. "Sue," he said.

"Suicide? Why would she—"

He shook his head. "Not suicide," he said. "Not suicide. I just—you know most of it by now anyway, don't you?"

"I don't know whether I know most of it, but I know enough to build on. I know enough to find out the rest. Asking you is just a shortcut."

He nodded, clasped and unclasped his hands, and stood again. "I've got to have a drink," he said. "Can I get you one?"

"No thank you," I said.

He tried to laugh. "No poison. Just Scotch and water."

"No thank you," I said.

He picked up the bottle from the middle of the dining room table and poured into the glass. It was Scotch only, no water.

"Are you drunk?" I asked.

"No. I wish I was." He drank from the glass, shuddered, and said, "You know the kind of thing I'd been mixed up in, with Curtis and Dan. Curtis always thought Sue didn't know about it, but she did, and she hated it. She—finally I decided she was right. I got out of it. I got a job. You know what I've been doing the last few years? Jeanne and Curtis didn't, but Sue did. I've been—driving a delivery route, putting panty-hose in stores in a twenty-county area. Pantyhose. Me. The great big hotshot soldier of fortune, selling pantyhose." He chuckled drily. "That sure wouldn't have paid for this house, would it?" He gestured around. "But I'd already paid for this house. You know what I paid for it with?"

"No," I said, "but I could venture a guess."

"You'd never in a thousand million years guess," he said. "I paid for it in human blood, maybe even American blood. Have you ever seen those announcements of government sales of scrap metal and so forth? Well, the truth is that a lot of stuff gets into those sales that isn't scrap at all. It's good stuff that nobody has the initiative to go and inventory. And you can get it for a little bit of nothing, at least in contrast to its real value. And you put together this bit from this sale and that bit from that sale, and pretty soon you've got a whole something. Something nobody meant to throw away or sell as scrap."

So far he wasn't telling me anything I didn't know, including the fact that I already knew he'd been involved. He fell silent. I just waited. He'd start talking again, eventually. In this kind of situation, whoever speaks first loses.

"Sidewinder missiles," he said then. "I managed to put together forty Sidewinder missiles. *Forty* of them. You know who I sold them to? Iraq. I sold them to Iraq. I sold them to Iraq before the Gulf War. Years before. I don't know if Iraq still had them by the time the war came along, or if they'd already used them, or if they'd sold them to somebody else. But I felt—you know what I felt like when the war happened and Iraqi missiles were hitting our troops and hitting Israel?"

He didn't wait for me to answer. He just went on bitterly, "I felt like the murderer I was. Up till then I'd managed to convince myself my hands were clean. It wasn't my fault the government decided to get rid of that stuff. My part was just entrepreneurial acumen. I was just making money, and I was making a lot of money. Sue and I—we hadn't wanted to have children. I guess I was greedy; I wanted all of Sue's time for me. I think—I don't know, I think maybe she did want children but she knew I didn't, and she saw how horrible a father Curtis was, and she didn't want to risk it. Kenneth—the kid always thought I hated him. I didn't. I don't. I just didn't want to be around him because—he made me feel like the selfish so-and-so I am. But anyway, when the missiles started falling—I finally listened to Sue. I said, 'All right, I'm out of this. Been there, done that. No more.' Curtis and Dan told me I could get out, but if they ever heard I'd ratted I was dead meat. Well, I knew that. They didn't need to tell me.

"You asked about Sue. How Sue died. A long time ago, while I was still in the business, Sue asked me what she was supposed to do if somebody official showed up while I was gone and started asking questions. She couldn't lie. You knew her. She never did know how to lie." He forced another chuckle.

"So I told her—I told her if that happened, go and take a handful of sleeping pills. I told her to be careful, that stuff can kill you if you're not careful. Call my pager—we had a number code that she would enter to warn me of trouble—and then take the sleeping pills. Take just enough to sleep until I had time to get home and take care of the problem.

"So I figure that's what she did. Only—she didn't know how many pills to take. That's all I can figure out; she didn't know how many pills to take. Or how many not to take. Or— maybe she took too many on purpose. I don't know.

"I was going to retire in another couple of years. I'd been promising that for ten years. Jam yesterday and jam tomorrow, but never jam today. I was going to retire. We were going to travel all over the world. She'd been looking forward to that; we'd been planning where-all we'd go, what-all we'd see. But planning, that's all we ever did, because—I had a lot more money than the IRS ever knew about, and if I started throwing it around too much they would one day notice. That's what they got Al Capone on, you know, income tax evasion. I wasn't going to let them get me. I told Sue that, and she told me there are places you can go, some of them nice places, that don't have extradition treaties with the United States. I told her just wait a little bit longer, we'd go. But I think the truth was I didn't know how to retire. I was afraid to retire. If I retired, I might have to get to know myself, and you know what? I think I knew I wouldn't like me very much, not if I got to know me very well. Anyway, Sue and I discussed 'what if' every now and then, and we always agreed on the same thing. She'd call my pager, she'd enter the code, and she'd take sleeping pills. But none of it was real. It was like a game we were playing. And then—Thursday, my pager gave me the code. I was in Corsicana when I got the signal. Corsicana, breeding ground of the world's most concentrated herd of fruitcakes. Real fruit-cakes. The Christmas kind. I think San Francisco is the breeding ground of the other kind. Anyway, I was in Corsicana, and I got the signal. And I went home. And you know what I found."

He began to sob again for a minute or two; then he drank from the glass again.

It was brutal to go on questioning him. I went on questioning him anyway. "Were you involved with that deal with the hijacked gasoline?"

"Which one? There've been several."

"The one where one of the drivers was killed."

"No," he said, "I was out of it by then."

"But you knew about it."

"I knew about it, yes."

"Did you know it was Santiago Ramirez who hijacked the trucks, who killed that one driver?"

"Yeah, I knew."

"Did you know a decent, honorable man with a wife and son went to prison for that crime?"

He stared at me. "No, I didn't know that. Curtis and Ellis didn't tell me, and I don't read newspapers very often, at least not local crime news. I used to keep track of what was happening in second- and third-world countries, because those were most of our markets, but now, not even that. Why do I need to know? I don't live in that world anymore."

"Well, now you do know," I said briskly. "And you're not going to sit there and drink yourself into a stupor. You're going to go take a shower and shave and put on clean clothes, and then you're going with me to the police station to make a formal statement so that man can get out of prison and go back home where he belongs."

"And how are you going to make me do that?" he asked, sounding genuinely puzzled.

"I don't have to make you do it," I said. "You're going to do it because you owe Sue that much honesty, at least."

"Ellis will kill me for it." But he was standing as he spoke, turning, leaving the bottle and glass behind him. "Not that I guess that matters anymore," he added.

"Oh, no, he won't," I said.

Ken turned back to stare at me. "Somebody killed Ellis?"

"Somebody killed Ellis."

"Who?"

"I'll just bet if you think about it long enough you'll guess. You had a telephone conversation yesterday, Sunday. I don't know what time, and I don't know what your side of the conversation was. But the person on the other end of the line said, 'But I couldn't let him go to prison.' And later she said, 'I didn't think. I should have realized but I just didn't *think.*'"

I've heard the expression that somebody looked pole-axed. I'd never before seen anybody who *really* looked pole-axed.

Then he said, very quietly, "Jeanne. Because what Jeanne did, she just thought she was keeping Curtis from going to prison. Ellis set her up. Ellis set me up too."

"How did he do that?"

"He called me from a phone booth. He told me one of his snitches had told him that there was a federal tap on his phone and Curtis's phone." (The snitch was premature; Dub had told me that there was not yet a tap on Ellis's phone.) "He told me he obviously couldn't call Curtis, not to mention the fact that he and Curtis had recently had a big blow-up, I think it was about Curtis selling shoddy merchandise when Ellis—he didn't mind being illegal, but he always delivered what he sold. There was something about some IRA guns, and Ellis was hopping mad over it. And on top of that, no matter what Ellis told Curtis about the FBI being on the trail, Curtis couldn't *do* anything about it. He told me to tell Jeanne that the feds were about ready to serve a search warrant there. He said that Curtis's computer was like a ton of dynamite; it would take down every one of us. He said for me to tell Jeanne that she was to arrange to have Curtis sleep late and her leave early some morning, and she was to leave the security system off, and he'd get in and take the computer. Then she was supposed to pretend the security system had been on, and pretend there'd been a burglary while she was gone and for some reason the alarm didn't go off."

"But the security system *was* on," I said.

"Trust Ellis to work around something like that. Anyhow—yeah, I knew. I knew he killed Curtis. I even knew how." He chuckled bitterly. "You know what he did? Curtis was on guard. He was always on guard. So Ellis chloroformed that dog and took off its collar. Then he crawled up the stairs jangling the dog collar, so if anybody—if Curtis, I mean—heard anything he'd just think it was the dog. Then he shot Curtis. Then he put the collar back on the dog—at least, he said he did." He looked at me. "But when I saw the dog later the collar was off."

"Ellis put it on twisted," I said. "So I took it back off. How did Curtis let you know, if you were out of touch? Do you have a cell phone?"

"No, just a pager. But I have voice mail on it. Anyway, then Ellis split. And he told me to get the stuff out of the safe."

"What did you think was in the safe?" I asked. "I heard Sunday afternoon you were over there yelling about something that was supposed to be there and wasn't."

"You talked to Kenneth, didn't you? The boy?"

"Never mind who I talked with. What did you think was in the safe?"

"Curtis kept some kind of written record. I didn't know what it was and I didn't know where he kept it, but Ellis told me to get it. One way or another, get it. It wasn't easy to search for it, not when I didn't even know what it looked like. I didn't ever find it."

"I know you didn't," I said. "The FBI has it."

Ken Rimer stared at me. Then, without saying anything else, he turned and walked out of the living room. A few minutes later I heard the shower running. It took him fifteen minutes to get back to me. He still smelled of booze, but he looked decent.

"What about Captain Millner?" I asked him in the car.

He shook his head. "I don't know anything about Captain Millner."

I took him to Millie, and we got a statement from him. I called Dub to tell him I had done so, and Dub asked me to ask Millie to fax a copy of the statement to his office. I did; then I took Ken back home.

By then it was after four, and I still had two more people to talk with. I didn't look forward to either of those conversations.

I went home.

# 2

$K$ENNETH WAS THERE. HE WAS ON THE COUCH, Ivory on his lap and Pat sitting beside him, and all three of them were intently watching *Wishbone*, which I considered one of the most delightful educational television series that I had seen in a very long time.

I sat down in my chair in the living room, and Kenneth got the remote, turned the television off, and looked at me. My expression must have warned him.

"What's wrong?" he asked.

"Mr. Ellis is dead," I said.

"Yeah? The same way as my dad?"

"Not exactly," I said. "Kenneth, I'm sorry, but I'm almost certain your mother killed him."

His face, which had always been pale, paled even more. After a long while, he said, "I suppose it's crummy of me to worry about myself right now."

"What's crummy about that?" I asked. "It's entirely reasonable for you to worry about yourself."

"It's just—I don't have any relatives. No grandparents, no aunts and uncles except Aunt Sue and she's dead, no cousins, *nobody*. So—if my mom goes to prison—where will I go?"

"What's wrong with right here?" I asked.

"You mean you'd let me? Even if—even if my mom killed your captain?"

That was a problem I hadn't wanted to think about, but he was right. I could figure out absolutely no way at all for anybody except Jeanne to have killed Captain Millner, but I also could figure out no reason at all for her to do it.

"Even then," I said. "You aren't either of your parents. You aren't responsible for what they do."

He hugged the dog again.

"I'm going out for a while again," I said. "When Harry gets home, tell him to go get Cameron. I'll make dinner when I get home."

# 3

---

I DIDN'T HAVE TO WORRY ABOUT SOMEONE getting there before me, because nobody else thinks quite the same way I do,
and I didn't know anybody else who by now would have put
the pieces together.

Anyway, I couldn't figure out how she got out of her
house, to Ellis's apartment, inside Ellis's apartment, and then
back home, considering that her house, throughout the entire
span of time during which Ellis could possibly have been
killed, contained not only her but also four police officers.

Until I could figure out how she did it, I wasn't ready to go
and confront her.

The problem was that without questioning her, I might
never figure out how she'd done it.

That meant I might as well go on and get it over with.

I parked the detective car in front of her house and went
and rang the doorbell.

Andrew Jackson opened the door. "Oh, hi," he said.

"Hi. Is Jeanne here?"

"She's around somewhere," he said. "I think up in her
room."

"Go and ask her if it's okay for me to go talk with her."

"Of course it's okay," he said, backing away from the door.
"Why wouldn't it be okay?"

"Please go ask her, Jackson," I said. "I'll wait right here."

He left. He returned a minute later. "She says yeah."

I entered and went up the stairs.

Jeanne's bed hadn't been made that morning. This, more than anything else that had happened, told me that she was falling apart; until this moment I had been convinced that she would get up out of her deathbed to make the beds and vacuum. She was lying on her back, covers drawn up to her waist, in the same clothes she'd been wearing when I saw her Sunday. Her eyes followed me as I went in and sat down on the chair beside the bed.

"You found him, didn't you," she said. It wasn't a question.

"Ellis? Yes, we found him. You know you don't have to talk—"

"Oh, shut *up!*" she said. "Do I have to hear that over and over and over and over and over? It's over. It's gone. All of it. Yes, I'll talk. What do you want to know? Ask me. I'll tell you. I just want to get it over with. I signed your paper the other day; I don't have to do it again, do I? I was trying to protect myself. I was trying to protect my child. I was even trying to protect my husband. That's a real laugh. Trying to protect him, I let in the man who killed him. Trying to protect my child, that's not a crime, but the things I did to do it, they were crimes, and don't think I didn't know it." She started crying. "What's going to happen to my son? He has nowhere to go—"

"He's at my house, Jeanne," I said, "and if you want, he can stay there."

"Even after what I did? Or do you have any idea what I did?"

"Even after what you did . . . you killed Ellis, and you killed Captain Millner. Yes, Jeanne, I did figure it out. All I need from you now are the details."

"I didn't mean to kill Captain Millner," she said. "I didn't. He—Ellis—he told me it would just put him to sleep a few hours. He didn't tell me it would kill him. I wouldn't have—Deb, I wouldn't have hurt your captain; he was a good man, and he was kind to me and to Kenneth, and not very many people have ever been. Kind to us, I mean. But—I was in so deep—I didn't know what to do. Ever. I just—it's like I've been a hamster on a treadmill ever since about six months after I married Curtis. Running and running and running and getting tireder and tireder and tireder, and never really getting anywhere at all. I—today I was even thinking, I was thinking maybe I should kill Kenneth and then myself, so he'd be safe. That's ridiculous, isn't it, to want to kill him so he'd be safe? And then I thought maybe I should kill you, because I didn't think anybody else could figure it out, and you're smart enough you could. But—what for? You've been kind to me and you've been kind to Kenneth. I—Deb—am I some sort of monster? I told you I sent Kenneth to school to get him away from Curtis. Well, that was part of it. But mainly—I—I couldn't stop thinking about it. That the only way to get out of the whole mess was to kill Kenneth and then kill myself. I let Curtis send him to school because when he was at school then I couldn't kill him. But I thought about it. I thought about it all the time."

I remembered Cubbins asking me just a few days ago, but as if it had been in another life, whether Jeanne had obsessive-compulsive disorder. I'd told him then that I didn't think so, at least not bad. But from what I was hearing now, I knew she did have OCD. Horrible, to think that sixty milligrams a day of Prozac could have stopped the entire downward spiral; could have given her what she needed to find the strength to take herself and Kenneth away, out of Curtis's clutches; could have allowed her and Kenneth to start new lives. Sixty milligrams a day of Prozac. She could have paid for it easily. But she didn't know she was ill. And neither did anybody else.

"Go on and tell me about it, Jeanne," I said. "Let's get it over with. You'll want to tell it all again at the police station so we can get it as a formal statement, but tell me first what happened. Tell me how you did it. That'll get you past the worst of it." And even as I was saying that, I was thinking, *Susan. Susan Braun, M.D., psychiatrist.* Susan had rescued my son-in-law Olead from what looked like schizophrenia and was really only a vitamin B imbalance. Susan could testify at Jeanne's trial; so could I. Susan could say that Jeanne was not responsible for her actions, as sick as she was. Susan had told me once when we were discussing OCD in relation to another case that it was 100 percent biochemical.

And Matilda. My friend Matilda Greenwood. She's a psychologist.

A person being treated for OCD needs medicine and emotional support. Susan would provide the medication, and Matilda and Susan both would supply the emotional support.

I didn't understand myself. I had been ready to turn and rend the person who killed my captain, but now that I knew who it was and why she did it, I could find no room within myself for anything but pity. The rage was gone. Captain Millner would understand that.

A ghost of a smile barely touched the corners of her pale lips. "Like taking off a Band-Aid. Let's get it over with."

"Like taking off a Band-Aid," I agreed.

She took a deep breath. "Okay," she said, and fell silent. After about three minutes she said, "Ken came over last Monday when I was working in the yard. He told me that Ellis had just called him and told him that there was a federal wiretap on our phone and Ellis's phone. He said Ellis had told him that there was enough information on Curtis's computer to put us all away for life, even Sue, and she didn't do anything. I didn't do much. Then, I didn't. Not before Thursday. He said I was to go call Ellis from a pay phone here, to a pay phone in Baltimore, at seven-fifteen in the evening my time on Tuesday.

"So I did. I called him, and he told me about the same thing Ken had told me. He told me—he told me to find a day when I could leave real early in the morning, before dawn. And you'd told me just a few hours before that you had to jog early on Thursday because you had to be in court. So I told him that. And he told me to tell him the security code, open the dining room window, leave a house key on the dining room table, and get out of there. He'd go in and steal the computer. You know"—she smiled briefly—"I didn't even *think* of the second computer. And he and Ellis had that big fight just before he got it, so of course Ellis didn't know about it.

"Then when I got home, I was going to discover the burglary. You know what I discovered instead."

"And that's why you kept saying it was your fault."

"It *was* my fault," she said. "I should have known Ellis well enough to know that. So—and the computer wasn't gone. The computer was right there. So the situation was worse instead of better—and then Kenneth showed up. That was when I realized Ellis planned to put the blame on Kenneth. Kenneth didn't run away from school on his own; Ellis put him up to it. And so I couldn't implicate Ellis. Ellis could testify where and when he'd dropped Kenneth off, and even Kenneth wouldn't know he'd dropped Kenneth there and then driven here, parked a block away, and come in the house while Kenneth was walking. And I didn't know what to do. And then Sue— why did she do it, Deb? I don't know why she did it."

"I've talked to Ken," I said, "and he told me it was an accident."

"How could it have been an accident? She had to have brought in the package from the mail; that makes it deliberate, doesn't it?"

"Not if she didn't know what a lethal dose was," I said. "All she wanted to do was sleep until Ken got back from Corsicana. She did it because she didn't know what else to do."

I wasn't really at all sure that was true. I'd worked a case once in which a woman deliberately committed suicide in a way that would frame someone for murder. I wasn't sure I wasn't seeing that again. But I wasn't sure who Sue would have tried to frame. Her husband? Jeanne? Ellis?

She hadn't swallowed a glass full of icky powders only half dissolved in water because she thought it would be fun. And I never did find out how she got the package containing Jeanne's heart medication from the mail.

But I'd let the medical examiner's office decide how Sue had died. It didn't fall under my job description, and right now I was glad it didn't.

Jeanne started nodding and forgot, for a time, to stop. Then she said, "I didn't know, then, why he didn't take the computer away the same time he killed Curtis. He told me later it was because I got back sooner than he thought I would. I don't believe that. I think he planned all along to kill Curtis and make it look like Kenneth did it, so I wouldn't tell anything for fear he'd put it on Kenneth.

"I don't know how he got back in to get the computer. He had a key; he had the security code; so all he had to do was walk in the door. But that wouldn't have been mysterious enough. He likes things to be mysterious; he likes things to be complicated. He came in through the dining room window somehow; he told me he was going to do it but not how, but I think one of your officers figured out how, and he—Ellis—took the computer away. He opened the safe at the same time. I don't know how he got that combination, unless maybe he got Ken to give it to him. I was—I was supposed to be sleeping on the couch. But I wasn't sleeping. I—I waited until Officer Raye went to the bathroom. Then I went in the dining room to tell Ellis, and he went across the hall to Curtis's office. Then I went back to pretend to be asleep. The next time Officer Raye went to the bathroom I told Ellis again, and he went back to the dining room. I don't know when he left. Officer Raye—I don't know if she told you. She told me. She's going to have a baby. And—she needed to go to the bathroom pretty often."

"No, she didn't tell me that," I said.

"Then on Saturday," Jeanne continued, "Ellis called me again. He told me the tap was off the phone, so he could talk freely." (*Dub's going to have to find and stop that leak,* I thought, *or none of their investigations will be secure.*) "He told me he'd seen the computer truck in front of the house, and he knew they couldn't be there about the office computer because he already had it. So he asked me, and that's when I remembered the second computer. Deb, I know it sounds ridiculous, but I really, honestly, had completely forgotten about the second computer."

"I'm not surprised," I said.

"Ellis was furious. He thought I'd done it on purpose. And then he thought the police were gone, so I could just hand him over the other computer. And I told him the police weren't gone. I told him about Captain Millner. He told me about some stuff—he didn't tell me what it was, and I don't know—but it was hidden in Curtis's office. It was a liquid in a little bottle, unlabeled. He told me where it was and how to get it, and he told me to pour it into Captain Millner's coffee and then call him when Captain Millner went to sleep.

"I almost didn't get a chance to do it, because Kenneth sat up for ages talking with Captain Millner. But finally he went to bed, and then I took some coffee in and told him—your captain—that I was going to bed, and there was plenty more coffee downstairs. I just brought him the one cup. And I had emptied the little bottle into it.

"I went back later, and he was asleep. I called Ellis, and he told me to put a loud movie on the VCR and leave it running, and then he came over and got the second computer and left again. And then—in the morning—I found your captain dead. And then I knew what I had done."

"How did you reach Ellis?" I asked. "Considering there were four police officers in your house?"

She smiled again. "I turned the alarm off, and then I let Polka out. Then nobody had any problem with my leaving it off, because sooner or later Polka would come back and want to come in, and nobody wanted to mess around with the security system just to let the dog in. I knew Polka would stay away a couple of hours, so while the alarm system was off I locked my bedroom door and then I went down the rope fire ladder I kept in Kenneth's room in case of fire. I walked over to Sue's house and used her car—she and I have copies of each other's car keys, in case one of us locks—locked—her keys in the car, and I used her pistol that Ken always wanted her to keep in the car. I didn't have any trouble getting Ellis to let me in. And—you know what? I'm not a bit sorry about killing him. I'm really not."

That didn't leave much to say.

I telephoned Gary, and I telephoned the district attorney, and then I went home and told Kenneth what had happened. I made barbecued chicken for supper.

Of course I didn't eat any of it.

I told Harry the Thursday Club was defunct, and I was never going to jog again, and I was going to go join the gym again and I didn't care how much it cost. He pointed out that he'd been telling me for years that I ought to rejoin the gym. Then he rubbed my back and told me to get some rest; he'd take care of the kids and kitchen.

Of course I cried myself to sleep.

# 4

---

HARRY TOOK THE DAY OFF. EVEN CAMERON didn't go to school. They, Lori, Kenneth, and I went to Captain Millner's funeral. There were a lot of people there that we knew, and one that I didn't. Ashraf Akhbar was standing with his wife and son. Nudara was standing four paces behind her husband—she would say, if I asked, that that was proper among her people—but her face was radiant. At least, as much of it as I could see was radiant.

I was wearing my uniform, complete with lieutenant's bars and a small gold-colored badge instead of the large chrome one I had worn so long. I had a narrow strip of black tape across the badge, as is proper among my people.

Captain Millner had asked a lot from me over the years. He'd expected a lot, and he'd gotten a lot.

This was the last thing he wanted me to do.

I couldn't not do it, now, could I?